SOUL OF THE HOME
Designing with Antiques

TARA SHAW

ABRAMS, NEW YORK

To my best friend and husband,
Robert Walsh

Contents

Introduction

Growing up, I had two strong role models in my mother and my grandmother, women who were very different from each other, but who both had one thing in common: fearlessness. Their homes reflected their disparate outlooks. My mother loved to paint and lined her walls with contemporary art; she was a minimalist and her furniture was—and still is—all white. I remember on Saturdays, we would walk around picking lint from the white carpet. My grandmother, on the other hand, was a world-class collector. Whether it was glassware, books, or fabrics, her desire to acquire knew no bounds. She had a highly organized fabric room filled to the ceiling with textiles of every imaginable geometry and color. She loved to sew and would make me clothes, so I had bespoke fashion from a very young age.

Both of these powerhouse women made an indelible impact on my life. They were risk takers, and constantly encouraged me to color outside the lines and walk through the walls of fear that spring up in life, which can be daunting for an adult, much less a child. I remember my grandmother once checking me out of school to help her pick out a new car. I selected a black fastback Mustang with a red leather interior. As we were driving home, she asked me to take the wheel—I was seven. Although I didn't know if I had the strength to press the brake and feared we might plunge into the river that bordered my grandparent's property, I never said a word about my trepidation because I did not want her to know I was terrified or think that I could not do what she asked me to do. It's a lesson that has served me all of my life, helping me to overcome many challenges and lead a life that was not exactly textbook normal; to get out of the boat and go way out into unknown waters; to trust that when doors opened, they opened for a reason.

One of those doors opened the day in 2000 when Jill Goodacre and Harry Connick Jr. called me and asked if they could come over to my house and talk about decorating their home in Connecticut. I had to lie down on the cold brick pavers that were in my galley kitchen after I hung up the phone. At the time, I was selling antiques and living in the second Victorian I'd purchased in New Orleans. The house had made the cover of *Veranda*, and my antiques warehouse at the Port of New Orleans had also been prominently featured. As I tried to explain to Goodacre and Connick, I wasn't a designer. I was an antiques dealer who spent five weeks at a time shopping in Europe and couldn't imagine having the bandwidth to devote the energy and time to a project like theirs. But when those two ask you to do something, it is irresistible.

I took on the project, and little by little, through more press and word of mouth, other work came in: renovation projects, ground-up builds, and a seven-story brownstone near Central Park in New York, as well as other endeavors in China, Estonia, and Greece. I was still an importer, but I was also becoming something else—a designer—and

more than anything, I was fascinated by how people lived their lives and how I could help them to do it beautifully, using antiques and furnishings to create the homes their hearts desired.

I could relate to that kind of desire. It was a similar passion—to find out who I was and how that might translate into my home—that led me to shop for antiques in Europe in the first place. The first twenty-foot container I shipped home to a mini storage space on Tchoupitoulas Street near the Port of New Orleans sold out in ten minutes. I couldn't believe my eyes. Eventually, that container led to more: sixteen forty-foot containers a year, filled with one-of-a-kind finds that I selected from markets, fairs, and dealers throughout Europe. I quickly learned it's what I was born to do. When I'm in Europe, I feel like a fish in water, driving through ancient villages, eating fair food, and appreciating every detail that an artisan has carefully carved to create a masterpiece centuries old.

I was starting to notice that reproduction furnishings were not what I was seeing firsthand in Europe. An idea I'd been toying with was creating a reproduction line that would feature the detail of carving and patina I always looked for in antiques but that would be attainable and affordable for the average consumer. Tara Shaw Maison was born.

I launched with forty-six items in 2007—right in the middle of a recession. Remarkably, it was an instant success. I worked in China intermittently for seven years, constantly monitoring the product to make sure the carving and manufactured patina stayed true to my vision of quality. By the end of that period, the Maison line had grown to over 260 items produced in seven factories in China, four in India, and additional locations in the United States. I had showrooms in High Point, North Carolina; New York; Atlanta; Dallas; and Las Vegas. That's when RH, then known as Restoration Hardware, approached me for a licensing deal. I filled a twenty-foot truck with Maison furnishings, shipped it to their headquarters, and my husband Robert (an attorney) and I flew to California for a meeting. While I continue to produce a small collection of TS Maison furniture with trusted artisans in New Orleans, a portion of the line was folded into the RH collection.

Years ago, I'd started writing *The Coat Your Father Gave You*, which I conceived as part spiritual guide, part memoir, based on the adventures I've been on and the lessons I've learned traveling and working throughout Europe and Asia. By chance at a party in New York I met book agent Jill Cohen, who suggested I write a book about my love affair with antiquity. I sent her my manuscript—you are holding the end result in your hands. Throughout my life, books have been indispensible teaching tools, spiritual guides, and invaluable methods of escape. There are stacks of them in nearly every room in my house, and without them, I'd never have been able to tell Louis XIII from Louis XIV, much less build an entire career on the love of antiques. My hope is that this volume is one such tool for you. I hope it helps you navigate through your own journey and that your journey is as rewarding, fulfilling, and beautiful as mine has been.

The Importance of Antiques

I t started with a desk. Or rather, an armoire. In 1998, I was working in the apparel industry with my own wholesale showrooms when I finally had enough money to invest in the kind of furniture I'd always admired in design magazines. An antique. Something one-of-a-kind, which only I would have. I figured if I bought well, I could probably afford one good piece a year. (My grandmother, who had a PhD in shopping, was the kind of person who would take me out of school to shop for pearls and go to shoe sales and the farmers' market. She drilled into me the concept of value. She was of the "buy the best and have no regrets" school, a trait she thankfully passed on to me, too.)

So I went shopping for what I thought I needed at the time: a desk for my home office, something elegant and sophisticated enough to compel me to do all my paperwork (and elevate what often felt like an unwelcome chore). I'd been a keen shopper for years, haunting antiques shops as I traveled from state to state for my work. The special thrill of a find that any inveterate shopper knows was very familiar to me. Even so, I was unprepared for the purchase that would change the course of my career, and actually, my entire life. One Saturday I walked into a store that was unloading a fresh shipment from Europe and there it was. Except it wasn't a desk at all. It was a gorgeous Louis XIV–XV armoire boasting a treasure trove of ravishing details: book-matched walnut doors painstakingly selected so the grain danced across their surfaces, a supremely elegantly carved cornice crowned with a swirling *coquille*, charming paw feet covered in a fading gilded wash. It stopped me cold. Something in all that beauty, in all that craftsmanship, in all that perfectly proportioned glory spoke to me, as if the artisan himself was reaching out across centuries to tap me on the shoulder and whisper *Take me home*. Like the ébéniste had made it just for me. I walked in looking for a desk, but I fell in love with an armoire and chose to follow my heart. In my experience, it's normally a bad idea to ignore the still, small voice inside that's giving you direction.

Painted Louis XVI chairs, a vintage Italian silver-leaf chandelier, and a vintage Italian *faux bois* table in my Port of New Orleans warehouse.

Antiques bestow an incomparable sense of history—something that's withstood the centuries is necessarily made extremely well. Their flaws, scrapes, and bumps are hard-earned and make your interiors (and maybe even you) more forgiving.

And that's it in a nutshell, why antiques are important, why they mean so much to me—that treasure-in-a-field moment. I could go on and on about how antiques bestow an incomparable sense of history—something that's withstood the centuries is necessarily made extremely well. Their flaws, scrapes, and bumps are hard-earned and make your interiors (and maybe even you) more forgiving. All of that is true. But that's not why I fell in love, and it's not why I changed career paths and still crisscross the globe, rising at ungodly hours and wearing out my wellies to fill forty-foot containers.

It's because an antique can seduce you in a way that no assembly-line-produced good ever could. And if you fill your environment with pieces that make you feel that way, then guess what? You're probably going to fall in love with your environment, too.

TOP, LEFT TO RIGHT: A nineteenth-century Swedish girandole, a type of candelabra. An eighteenth-century Italian gilded console boasts whimsical carved faces on its legs. The escutcheon, or keyhole, on a nineteenth-century, Louis XIV–XV-style commode. The intricately carved back of a nineteenth-century Italian chair. MIDDLE, LEFT TO RIGHT: An eighteenth-century gilded rococo mirror. A Gustavian bench and *mouchoir* jardinière. A seventeenth-century statue of a soldier. A Gustavian tall case clock. BOTTOM, LEFT TO RIGHT: Eighteenth-century gilded Italian candlesticks and a nineteenth-century Louis XVI-style mirror. A carved and painted eighteenth-century Italian *pot au feu*—flaming pot—architectural fragment. A vintage Italian rock crystal chandelier. A neoclassical motif is carved into the top of a nineteenth-century French trumeau (or mantel mirror).

Starting an Antiques Collection

If you're new to the world of centuries-old furniture, you might not know how to begin collecting. Well, when I started doing this more than twenty years ago, neither did I. I was terrified of making a mistake. I could only afford to buy one good piece a year and I had to make it count.

As I explained in the previous chapter, that first time I went out looking for a desk—a Louis XVI one, to be precise—but instead surprised myself by coming home with a gorgeous but unusual armoire that was actually transitional Louis XIV–XV. It had some of those strong, clean lines I was looking for, but also prominent rococo and masculine details associated with those earlier eras, and somehow encapsulated the casual elegance I wanted to live with. The purchase was seminal, leading the way for my subsequent acquisitions—a Louis Philippe commode (chest), a pair of neoclassical bronze-urn lamps, a footed nineteenth-century painted Italian console—that all either complemented or contrasted with the qualities I originally fell in love with in the armoire and slowly began to establish the laid-back refinement I sought for my home.

All that is to say that there's no science to it. You've got to feel your way, taking one step at a time and letting each new purchase bring its own note to the symphony. Of course, you should still do your homework. Soak in all the info you can get your hands on: coffee-table and reference books, auction catalogs, magazines, the Internet, and social media apps like Instagram. Beyond reading about antiques, expose yourself to as many antiques as possible. Start at the top, with museums, to see blue-chip pieces in historic settings. Round out that exposure with flea markets and shops where you'll be able to touch furniture: open drawers, inspect joints, and get a feel for finishes and woods that appeal to you. It will all make for a fascinating education, I promise.

Bearing all those resources in mind, the style overview in this chapter is not meant to be the be-all and end-all of reference works. What it is designed to do is familiarize you with the broad characteristics of the eras and styles I turn to again and again, give you insight into why I use them repeatedly, and share a few pointers on how you might best incorporate them into your own style and home. Which of the several Louis periods—XIII, XIV, XV, or XVI—suits you best? How much character can you expect from Italian pieces? What will a nice Swedish find do for your living room? And don't feel like you have to box yourself in to just one genre. As you'll see throughout this book, I think mixing pieces from different eras and countries is the most beautiful approach when it comes to decorating a home—and I'll share how I do that, too.

A gilt Louis XIV mirror retains both its original mirror glass and cornice, a rare find because the cornice and frame were always carved separately then joined together and seldom survived centuries without getting a divorce (note how the distinctive crosshatch pattern on the cornice continues on the frame). Aside from the glass's telltale cloudy appearance (which, keep in mind, can be faked), a tap on its surface with the tip of your fingernail will yield a dense sound in a lower pitch than you'd get from modern glass.

LOUIS XIII & LOUIS XIV

The Louis eras in design—XIII through XVI—roughly correspond to the reigns of those respective French kings. The first eras among them, Louis XIII and XIV, are similar enough that they can be grouped together, and in contemporary decorating they often get passed over. These are not antiques known for subtlety. When compared to the lilting and sculptural forms that came in the later Louis eras, they can often feel heavy and immovable. But that was the point. The two kings reigned during tempestuous political times and spent much of their time consolidating power, filling their palaces with furniture that communicated it.

What you'll get with Louis XIII and Louis XIV, unsurprisingly, are strong, upright silhouettes. Louis XIII forms tend to have straight lines while Louis XIV pieces exhibit some subtle curves. Seating will have turned or carved legs and stretchers, wide seats, and broad seat backs that happen to have very comfortable pitches—which is what I like about them. A Louis XIII or XIV chair is great for a home office, or as an extra seat in the living room. I call them manly chairs because they have a scale that men particularly like.

In later Louis XIV pieces you do begin to see a bit of the scrolling movement that presages the rococo proportions to come—especially in the arms and the stretchers known as *os de mouton*, which literally translates as "sheep bones" and is an apt description of their shape. The main takeaway from these two Louis styles is that a little goes a long way. One or two pieces in an interior will add highly functional variety without overpowering a scheme.

TOP, LEFT TO RIGHT: A wider view of a rare Louis XIV gilded mirror with its original glass shows its substantial scale, a Louis XIII and XIV hallmark. Eighteenth-century Tuscan candelabras and a gilded Louis XIV armchair are beginning to anticipate the curvy shapes of the rococo and Louis XV eras. Notice the scrolling stretcher known as an *os de mouton*, or "sheep bone" on the armchair. You can see why I call these pieces manly chairs: They're wide, comfortable seating options that no one will be afraid to sit in. MIDDLE, LEFT TO RIGHT: I love the Louis XIII side chairs, probably Spanish, for their elaborately carved and gilded stretchers and finials: Add a pair like this to a living room and it'll provide instant interest. On first glance, an eighteenth-century Italian sconce seems like it belongs to the Louis XV period (those curves!), but it's a transitional Louis XIV-XV piece with an erect, sturdy profile, and thus bears marks of more than one style, common for pieces that span two eras. The same is true for the Louis XIII-XIV desk, with its upright, turned legs (Louis XIII details) and curling stretcher and apron (Louis XIV touches). BOTTOM, LEFT TO RIGHT: The Louis XIII table is a case study for the period with a clean-lined stretcher, straight, turned legs, and the simple construction typical of the era. The legs and stretchers of the Louis XIII chair illustrate the same characteristics. The eighteenth-century coffre (chest) is a painted Italian version of the Louis XIV style.

LOUIS XV

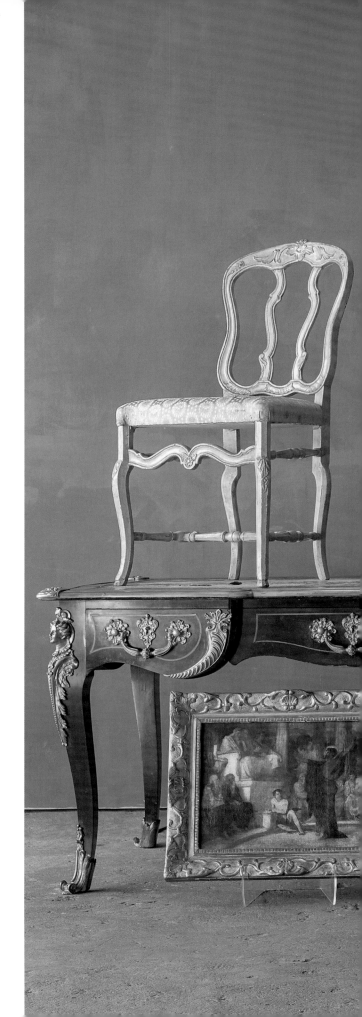

As Newton said, for every action, there is an equal and opposite reaction, and the stolid forms of Louis XIII and XIV produced a graceful response in Louis XV. Stylistically, the middle of the eighteenth century in France is characterized by the rococo style: a taste for flowing, elegant lines, asymmetry, and nature-inspired motifs like the *coquille,* or shell. In other words, the opposite of everything that came before.

When it comes to furniture, forms and silhouettes are dominated by S and C curves. You'll see scrolling arms, aprons, cornices, and cabriole legs ending in snail-shell curlicues. Carving will have leaves and flowers and sometimes ribbons. Applied decoration like lacquer, marquetry, and inlay was perfected into an art form. This is the classic look of French interiors, what we all think of when we imagine a proper Paris salon.

Unsurprisingly, Louis XV antiques pack a healthy dose of romance. Whereas the Louis XIII and XIV styles feel overtly masculine, Louis XV pieces are unapologetically feminine. They're fluid, lyrical, and so poetic: perfect for bedrooms and dressing rooms. A Louis XV armoire is aces at anchoring a corner of the living room (and hiding the TV and other electronics). You can also play up or down the glamour quotient with upholstery: A bright silk velvet will up the ante on an armchair, while a nubby, neutral linen will tone the whole thing down.

The armoire on the right is the first piece I ever bought (even though I went out looking for a desk!). You can see what captivated me: book-matched walnut doors (the graining matches), a cornice and apron with scrolling *coquille* details and gilding. But it's likely a transitional piece—it has some details, like carved animal feet, more typical of Louis XIV. The armchair and side chair are classic Louis XV: Notice the curving cabriole legs and the shell at the top of the seat back. The armchair is the grand dame here—I'd put her in a bedroom or living room, while the little foot soldier side chair is a shoo-in for a breakfast or dining room. The vintage chandelier, a modern piece, captures everything that's beautiful about Louis XV and is a testament to the style's enduring appeal. The *bureau plat*—or desk—is a showstopper with a red, tooled-leather top, bronze fittings, and graceful cabriole legs capped with decorative sabots. I've used pieces like this in very contemporary settings with everything else toned down to let them really attract attention. I included the painting because of its frame. With shells, scrolls, and the suggestion of asymmetry, it has it all, with gilding to boot.

SWEDISH

Much like the Italians, the Swedes adopted French forms and then painted them—but while the Italians used bright tones and plenty of gilding to embellish their furniture, their Nordic counterparts took a more somber approach, sticking to pale shades of ivory, gray, and blue. This makes sense when you consider they were looking to lighten interiors that saw very little sunshine during half the year. The neutral colors reflected that precious commodity and helped extend its impact indoors.

Northern interiors also tended to be less ostentatious than those in sunnier climes, so Swedish pieces can have a plainspoken nobility to them that, when paired with their distinctive finishes, makes them exceedingly easy to incorporate into modern spaces. They bring an incredible amount of depth to a room, but in a very subtle way.

Pieces from the Gustavian era—named for the king who reigned in the late eighteenth century, roughly during the same time as Louis XVI—are the most famous of Swedish antiques and boast the elegant neoclassical lines popular during that era. Those clean and simple proportions only add to their versatility. But even earlier rococo pieces—those that echo Louis XV shapes—can also be very sculptural, and are just as friendly to contemporary life.

FROM TOP, LEFT TO RIGHT: A unique Gustavian trumeau features a bust medallion of King Gustav himself, and gilt details rare in a Swedish piece. Cream paint in the background of the frieze accentuates the gilded carving. Nineteenth-century demilune tables are more typical of Swedish pieces: graceful and elegant, but humble. They're so useful as bedside tables, flanking a fireplace in a living room, or pushed together in a foyer to form a round table. An eighteenth-century sofa bench features exquisite carved arrow stretchers, a beaded apron, and neoclassical legs. As elaborate as the carving is, the painted finish tones everything down—it's so approachable! Which is not to say you can't use a piece like this to make a statement. Cover the same settee in bright silk taffeta and suddenly you've got something unforgettable. I treat tall case clocks like this eighteenth-century version as sculpture—good for anywhere you want to highlight ceiling heights because its slim profile draws the eye up. Eighteenth-century stools are another convenient form: great for the foot of the bed or as extra seating in a dining room. The eighteenth-century armchair is a Swedish version of a French marquis (the term for an extra-wide armchair). The stretcher on the back is necessary for structural support—and an extra opportunity for details like a carved wheat-sheaf motif.

EMPIRE

The French Empire period coincides roughly with Napoleon's rule in the early nineteenth century. It's another neoclassical style, but like those of Louis XIII and XIV, it was meant to idealize the French state, so it can lack some of the delicacy of Louis XV and XVI. It embraced opulence and imperial grandeur, with motifs like crowns, *N* and *J* initials (for Napoleon and Josephine), swans, bees, and Egyptian iconography (reflecting the emperor's exploits in Egypt). Tables with claw feet were in style along with saber-legged chairs and columns on case goods—all correlating to movements in nineteenth-century architecture and furniture.

While Empire pieces do tend to feel heavier, I like them because they're typically made of beautiful wood, and most of the case goods and mirrors will have column details, which I love. The Empire style is pared down enough that it mixes well with contemporary furnishings, and Empire commodes and armoires are wonderful in bedrooms (I have one in mine).

Lighting is another Empire strong suit. Chandeliers have all the neoclassical bells and whistles, but they tend to feel minimal and elegant, making them very versatile and not at all overpowering. Those with tole rings and baskets of crystal have tall, lean profiles, so they work well in spaces with high ceilings—they're sensational in a soaring dining room over a modern minimalist table.

TOP, **LEFT TO RIGHT:** An Empire-style Italian chandelier boasts everything I love about lighting in this period: crystal baskets suspended from original tole rings and tole bobeches. It's delicate but has a long silhouette, so it would tame a lofty space. I'll always go for a handsome Empire case piece like this commode—plainspoken but still boasting details like the bone column capital and original hardware. The tole swan urn on a pedestal exhibits a favorite motif of the Empress Josephine's. **MIDDLE, LEFT TO RIGHT:** A swan motif is also evident on the sloped back armchair with saber legs. A brass and marble top coffee table is vintage but boasts Empire details such as claw feet. **BOTTOM, LEFT TO RIGHT:** The Empire-style daybed illustrates another asset of the period: rich woods, in this case, veneer mahogany. The unusual Empire tole chandelier is a conversation piece and would probably work best in a setting where everything else is extremely well edited. With caryatid legs and claw feet, the gilded oval table is resplendent, reprising classical motifs from Greek architecture.

MIDCENTURY

I bet you didn't think you'd find space devoted to twentieth-century vintage pieces in a book about antiques, did you? The truth is, I think sticking to any one era can date an interior. And even though midcentury pieces were mass-produced or machine-made, many of them were nevertheless based on ancient forms, with all the frills stripped out. That Mies van der Rohe daybed on the right embodies a silhouette that goes back to ancient Egypt, so there's a thread that connects it to something neoclassical like the straight lines of a Louis XVI bench or chair. On first glance they have nothing to do with each other, but take a deeper look and you start to understand that they actually have a lot in common. They're striving for a similar simplicity and grace. And, since they approach that goal very differently, what you'll get in exchange is electricity.

In terms of materials, midcentury pieces will also give you a break from the brown wood that dominates the antiques world. Which doesn't mean that they have to be slick: The pieces I gravitate towards employ tactile ingredients like leather, iron, and steel. And if the finishes are not pristine, even better. Cracked leather and slightly flaking chrome will get along all the better with a chalky eighteenth-century Swedish finish or an Italian piece with chipping gilt.

Here's another good reason to like midcentury: Practically speaking, since midcentury pieces were industrially produced, there tend to be a lot of them and they can be good deals in fairs and markets.

I used a 1503 Italian ecclesiastical portrait as a backdrop prop to show you how well midcentury pieces can play with an object that predates them by four hundred years. How striking does that Corbusier chaise look in front of it? With its leather and heavy cotton upholstery and matte black base, the chaise has enough texture to stand up to the weathered work of art. The Savonarola chair on the daybed is a modern version of seating popular during the Renaissance—the same time period as the portrait—so the leap through time and space is not coming totally out of left field. Those kinds of through lines are the key to mixing and mingling pieces from different periods. The occasional table on the far left shows off overtly neoclassical references in its arrow legs. The chandelier is by Swedish designer Erik Höglund; even though it's modern, the crystal drops feature dimensional impressions so they have wonderful character. The Mies van der Rohe daybed is just another iteration of an age-old formula, and it's so functional—I love daybeds in any room, really, because they add extra seating without visually cluttering the space. The midcentury Spanish starburst mirror is a showpiece for over a bed or to anchor a powder room or foyer—the detail of even the smallest object plays a key role in the depth of design.

Antiques show their age
and history, blemishes
and all. That kind
of imperfection is a lovely
thing to live with
because it's so forgiving.
It's just what I want
to come home to.

A Collector's Sanctuary

I'm going to let you in on a little secret. When it comes to my own home, as incredible as it sounds, I'm a modernist at heart. I don't like clutter, frilliness, or anything overly precious. What antiques give me is authenticity. They show their age and history, blemishes and all. That kind of imperfection is a lovely thing to live with because it's so forgiving. It's just what I want to come home to.

Though my house was inspired by a château the previous owner saw in France, it was built fairly recently. It's a modern residence cloaked in graceful bones, just my style. Foremost it's functional, with private areas that feel like havens and public areas that bend easily for either one-on-one meals with my husband or dinner parties for a crowd.

Loving old things doesn't mean your house has to look stuck in the past. My design philosophy has always been to seek out the one-of-a-kind pieces that speak to me, and then edit, edit, edit. You have to pare things down to give your collected pieces the spotlight. In my living room alone, there are several standout objects—a Louis XIII–XIV armoire; a Gustavian daybed with a weathered finish; a gilt eighteenth-century Italian altarpiece turned into a cocktail table—but I pulled back stylistically on nearly everything else. All the upholstery is neutral, with just the tiniest dose of pattern on pillows. The windows are bare, and sisal or cowhide rugs are unobtrusive splashes of texture on the floor. In my bathroom, I covered the walls in salvaged Louis XV paneling with a faded verdigris patina, and converted a console and mortar, both eighteenth century, into a vanity and sink. The bathtub, however, is contemporary, the floors are simple honed marble, sharp chrome sconces flank the vintage Venetian mirror, and, as in the living room, the entire palette sticks to shades of white.

Take it from me, if you're committed to collecting, give up on the idea that your interiors will ever be "done." It's self-evident when you really think about it—would you wear the same exact outfit for the rest of your life? Why would you want your house to? You'll buy a new piece and need to fit it in somewhere and you'll have to move things around—and that's OK. You'll keep what you like and readjust what you don't, and as a result, the spaces you inhabit will live and breathe and evolve. What you'll be left with is a house that never stops reflecting who you are and who you've been, all while saving room for what you'll become. Doesn't that sound gorgeous?

OPPOSITE: Brother Lucca, our whippet, standing guard in the rear yard. A French finial flanks the corner of the pool. PRECEDING PAGES: When I bought the property, I planted about fifty trees that are pruned into a formal French style, except for the wisteria I let tangle into the iron gate for a sense of mystery. One of the major statements in the foyer is an eighteenth-century gilt and painted chandelier; the eighteenth-century wood plinth—one of two pieces I own that have the Medici family crest—holds a nineteenth-century cast-iron jardinière.

My design philosophy
has always been to seek
out the one-of-a-kind pieces
that speak to me,
and then edit, edit, edit.
You have to pare things
down to give your collected
pieces the spotlight.

OPPOSITE: Under antique and vintage chargers, flatware, and stemware, a tablecloth would feel like too much, so I like to leave the wood of a Gustavian-style table bare. The marble sculpture on the console is by David Lapin. PRECEDING PAGES: An eighteenth-century Swedish buffet and bench give weight to the other side of the dining room where a nineteenth-century painting from the Genoese school holds court and is an unexpected juxtaposition to the contemporary sculptures. Glossy paint on the floors and walls of the dining room, along with hand-laid tea paper ceilings, creates a glamorous backdrop for antiques in chalky finishes, including eighteenth-century Swedish chairs and a dining table based on an original I sold. I paired a florid eighteenth-century painted French console with a neoclassical cast-concrete molding I turned into a mirror—an unexpected duo that works really well thanks to texture and color. The ceramic sculptures, by Evelyn Jordan, are a contemporary riff on those same themes that brings the entire room firmly into the twenty-first century.

RIGHT: The pecky cypress-lined library is my home office where I turned a nineteenth-century painted Italian table into a desk. The gilded eighteenth-century Italian candelabra disguises any tabletop clutter from the doorway. I topped the vintage Italian secretary with an eighteenth-century reliquary in a faux marble finish to give it extra height and emphasize the room's lofty proportions. The Louis Philippe daybed and the vintage Arne Norell chair and ottoman are extra seating for reading and relaxing.

PRECEDING PAGES: The foyer sets the scene for the rest of the house with a Richard Serra screen print, a fragment of a seventeenth-century statue, a Louis XV gilt mirror, and an eighteenth-century gilded console carved with the Medici family crest.

THE ONES THAT DIDN'T GET AWAY

I have shopping in my DNA and also shop for a living, so if I didn't set certain limits on what I allow myself to buy for my own home, I might go out of business. I call them my "ones"—for every shipping container I fill on a European shopping trip, I get to keep one thing. Since I'm trying to be discerning and only buy things I'll never see again in the first place, my ones can be pretty spectacular, at least to me (which is the point, as I'll explain below): a gilded eighteenth-century Italian console with carved faces I suspect once belonged to the Medicis that greets people in my foyer; a monolithic nineteenth-century Genoese school painting of Jesus in the garden of Gethsemane that dominates the dining room; a charming collection of mounted and framed blown eggs that's like a series of Joseph Cornell shadow boxes for which I still haven't found the right place (trust me, I will).

Considering all the "ones" I've bought—and luckily, my house is filled with them—I'm proud to say I've never once suffered from buyer's remorse. The opposite, however, is definitely true. Sometimes, for whatever reason, a certain piece didn't rise to the level of a "one" for me and I'd unpack it from the shipping container and prop it in the warehouse and pray it wouldn't sell, because I knew I might never see another one like it. I've had my heart broken several times that way, watching that kind of thing go out the door with someone who saw in it exactly the allurement that I did.

All of which is to say that the number one rule of antiques shopping is buy what you love. Don't worry about where you're going to put it or how it will get along in the living room or whether it will complement the painting in the dining room. I promise that acquisition is better than remorse. Learn how to recognize that moment in which you connect to an item and then commit. Even now, after more than twenty years at it, I'm constantly working on upgrades—and hope to be for the rest of my life.

OPPOSITE: Follow your heart and you can't go wrong. A selection of the "ones" I bought for myself includes (from top, left to right) a Louis XIII–XIV armoire, an eighteenth-century Swedish rococo bench and clock, a footed nineteenth-century Italian occasional table, an eighteenth-century Flemish tapestry, an eighteenth-century plinth painted with the Medici family crest, a framed collection of blown eggs, a decorative urn, and a Louis XV commode with original hardware. PRECEDING PAGES: Vellum books, opera glasses, prayer books, and magnifying glasses are some of the other things I collect; the chair is Louis XIII.

I used a plainspoken but beautiful Gustavian farm table in the kitchen's breakfast nook and paired it with a clock and *encoignure*, or corner cabinet, all from the same era. Contemporary leather chairs by Mario Bellini and cast-concrete stools, as well as an extravagant Louis XIV chandelier, mean the scene isn't stuck in any one time period.

Corner cabinets like the Swedish model (*above*) and the Venetian example (*right*) were usually purpose-built for specific spaces, but can be convenient as storage pieces in rooms with tight proportions. Keys with burlap tassels serve as handles to pull open doors and complement worn finishes.

ELEVATING THE ORDINARY

Like many people, I have things on my design to-do list that I haven't yet gotten around to and foremost among them is renovating my kitchen. On its face, there's nothing really wrong with it—since the house is fairly new, it's functional and has served its purpose well since the day I moved in, which is probably why it's taking me so long to address what I dislike about it. My main quibble is that, left alone, it's a standard builder's space without much warmth or personality. The floors and cabinetry especially—two of a kitchen's major design elements—don't reflect my style or my point of view.

But since I knew I'd have to live with it for a while, I did need to make it feel more like me until I have the time and budget to make the cosmetic changes that I want. Unsurprisingly, I did this with antiques.

To combat the somewhat sterile atmosphere imparted by the ordinary surfaces, I needed to introduce pieces that went in the opposite direction. I filled the space above the fireplace with a nineteenth-century decorative urn beautifully carved from solid wood—it was one of my "ones." It has a striking, flaking-paint-and-wood patina and a swag drapery, which gives the minimal stone fireplace both architecture and age.

I also got creative with the lighting, forgoing standard pendants in favor of eighteenth-century Italian rococo lanterns with visible repairs (I love those, too) and gorgeously warm gilt finishes showing scattered losses. They just exude history and romance. Hung above the island, they instantly transformed the space.

Furnishings and accessories did the rest of the work to get the room to feel like the rest of the house. A thickly knotted sisal rug makes part of the floor feel tactile. A klismos-style chair is a place to park my handbag while I'm going in or out and has a forged iron frame, just like the bases of the shapely stools I pulled up to the counter, bringing in an earthy, masculine note. An enormous stone mortar dominates one end of the counter—a familiar form in a blown-out scale that makes a statement with a wonderfully rough-hewn texture earned over hundreds of years. It makes for a perfect beverage cooler at parties.

I upgraded a standard builder's kitchen with a few key antiques, including a nineteenth-century decorative urn, eighteenth-century Italian rococo lanterns, and a monumental stone mortar.

An eighteenth-century Swedish armchair and rococo sofa bench turn the second-story landing into a destination in and of itself. The eighteenth-century painted and gilded chest is a handy space to store blankets in summer. The French wooden plinth and Italian etched marble garden urn are both nineteenth century.

Give up on the idea that your interiors will ever be "done." It's self-evident when you really think about it—would you wear the same exact outfit for the rest of your life? Why would you want your house to?

Commodes like this Louis XVI version in the master bedroom are excellent bedside tables because they offer storage underneath and lots of space for bedside essentials—lamps, books, boxes—on top. The mirror is an eighteenth-century Italian rococo piece that provides much of the drama in the room.

A nineteenth-century plinth holding a vintage garden urn is silhouetted dramatically in my bedroom, a reference to the garden beyond and the fact that my husband and I call the space our tree house. The vintage cast-concrete column lamp picks up a theme in the nineteenth-century neoclassical sofa bench, which has fluted legs. When I bought the Empire armoire it was missing both of its exterior column details, so I had my furniture restorer create new ones to match. The vintage Savonarola chairs mimic the lines of the Louis XIII chair, my go-to for bedrooms.

I favor canopy beds with clean-lined proportions because they feel like havens without overtaking the space and let the antiques take the spotlight. The two-tone bed frame is a refreshing modernist pop in an antiques-filled space; mine was partially painted to match the walls so it doesn't feel completely out of place. The framed art on the walls is a collection of miniature friezes—Grand Tour-era copies from classical sites. The eighteenth-century Swedish gilt bench is covered in a neutral but iridescent velvet—not too loud to detract from the palette but strong enough to stand up to a gold finish.

Even switching out something as minor as chairs—the upholstered pieces here in exchange for the Savonarolas in previous pages—can change the tenor of a room. I'm always reconfiguring arrangements like this, working through the process of balancing everything until it feels right. A house should never definitively be "done." The cocktail table is covered in high-gloss paint as a counterpoint to matte finishes elsewhere. The curtains are made from a polished Italian cotton—substantial, but still ethereal.

ABOVE: A contemporary wallpaper on the stair landing can be seen from the foyer and, on first glance, looks like a work of art; those kinds of surprises keep interiors vibrant and interesting. The stools are nineteenth-century Italian. OPPOSITE: An eighteenth-century clock secretary in the guest room gives visitors a place to work. PRECEDING PAGES: I designed the entire master bathroom around salvaged Louis XV paneling with a wonderful patina and kept many of the other elements subdued so the room wouldn't feel like a French period re-creation. The only other standout piece is a vanity I had made from an eighteenth-century French painted console with an eighteenth-century mortar as a sink; I paired it with an eighteenth-century Swedish barrel-back chair.

As the major style imprint in bedrooms, the bed plays an important role. In this guest space, a striking Empire model with gilded caryatid finials sets up a refined and unexpected atmosphere. A close pair of gilt Gustavian trumeaus and bits of gilding still evident on the eighteenth-century Swedish lyre-back chair help the space coalesce. A Louis XVI chaise is upholstered in linen to match the bedding and curtains and lighten the rest of the room.

ABOVE: The back garden is screened with thirty-foot-tall Savannah hollies, which make the entire space feel like a secret escape. **OPPOSITE:** A blend of vintage and nineteenth-century garden statues and urns make the property seem as if it's been there forever. **PRECEDING PAGES:** Outdoor tables extend the dining room outside in warm weather. The nineteenth-century statue stands guard over the pool.

Always feather your nest
with things that are
meaningful to you. You
should be able to
"read" a great house just
like a biography.

RIGHT: For a couple that entertains often, the living room is a showcase with a few key statement pieces. The nineteenth-century Italian credenza, eighteenth-century Italian altar (repurposed as a cocktail table), Tom Corbin bronze statue, and painting by Adele Sypesteyn are the standouts, so everything else is toned down, with low, contemporary seating and chairs (gilt arms are a nod to the antiques) and a neutral color scheme. Walls are covered in a beige grass cloth for a hint of subtle texture, and floor-to-ceiling silk curtains add a charismatic glow. **PRECEDING PAGES**: In the foyer, out-of-the-box form follows function as a nineteenth-century stone-topped butcher table, nineteenth-century French lyre-back chairs, and an Empire trumeau provide a landing place for keys, mail, and last-minute checkups in the mirror. Though they represent different styles and are from disparate eras, the table and chairs work together because they share the lyre motif. An Italian candelabra and nineteenth-century Italian processional batons are the sort of one-of-a-kind accessories that add character to a new home.

To take advantage of lakeside views, a modern addition with glass walls was built as a true living room. Architectural features like Doric columns, coffered ceilings, and a Louis XV-style fireplace and mantel help connect it to the rest of the house. Furnishings in pairs—contemporary sofas, ottomans, and armchairs, Italian torchères and candlesticks—give a space instant cohesion.

Combine things with an eye to shape and silhouette—straight-backed Louis XIII dining chairs and a rectilinear Bulthaup cooktop and hood—and it won't necessarily matter that they were created centuries apart. Wipe-clean leather upholstery makes spills and splatters irrelevant. To establish a carefree, friendly environment, a nineteenth-century iron base was topped with new marble to create the table. The eighteenth-century Italian chandelier and corona soften all the stainless steel.

Bedrooms are a retreat
from the rest of the house—
and the world—and there's
something incomparably
comforting about canopy
beds. Instant safe haven.

A reproduction canopy bed with a cornice and curtains in the master bedroom is a lifetime piece that can easily be updated with new upholstery. The nineteenth-century tole and velvet chest provides extra storage and is a practical alternative to the standard bench. Other antiques include a pair of Tuscan Louis XIII-style armchairs, and an eighteenth-century gilt mirror and French commode.

ABOVE: A vanity in the dressing room adjoining the master bathroom is composed of a nineteenth-century French mirror, an eighteenth-century gilded Italian Louis XIV–style chair, a vintage iron torchère, and a contemporary Plexiglas table. **OPPOSITE:** Incorporating furnishings that are normally reserved for a living room, like a contemporary chaise and occasional table, will help turn a bathroom into a haven that provides alternative spots for checking email or sipping morning coffee. The folding screen in front of the window can be pulled closed for privacy without blocking out natural light. Floors and walls partially covered in marble are a serene but luxe backdrop.

LUSH LIFE

When I design bedrooms, I like to think of them as refuges. They're the innermost sanctums and a retreat from the rest of the house—and even the world. To that end there are elements I use to furnish that kind of escape.

Foremost among them is a canopy bed, usually a simple contemporary version forged of thin lengths of iron. Stylistically, they emphasize ceiling heights without drawing too much attention to themselves—normally it's the antiques that I want to let shine. Secondly, they create cocoon-like spaces where you can feel cossetted. There's something incomparably comforting about them. Instant safe haven. For extra sumptuousness, place a rug under the bed—sheepskin, knotted silk, Berber wool—so when you step out of it there's something soft underfoot.

Chests are practical as bedside tables if you have the room. They're perfect for storage but I love the real estate they can provide for lamps, books, and boxes to hide remote controls and glasses. Next is a mirror, necessary for dressing and getting ready but also useful for opening up smaller spaces. Antique or vintage Venetian is always lovely and an eighteenth-century silver- or gold-gilt framed option even lovelier.

Extra seating is a must and this is no time for dainty side chairs. You want something ample and comfortable, so it functions as an alternative place to read, pull on boots, or accommodate a significant other for a chat or a drink while you make the bed or finish getting ready for dinner. Louis XIII or XIV armchairs are my go-to, but I also love wide-seated Louis XVI or Swedish versions. If you have room, add a cocktail or occasional table so there's somewhere to set a book or drink down.

This guest bedroom has all the components of a sanctuary. The nineteenth-century painted Venetian mirror and silk taffeta curtains furnish an enchanting vibe. A nineteenth-century Louis XVI–style settee and custom bench provide ample seating, and an eighteenth-century Italian commode gives visitors a place to unpack. A canopy bed with lithe lines creates a retreat-within-a-retreat and doesn't draw too much attention from the antiques. A contemporary work by Jean Geraci makes the room fresh and current.

A shapely and substantial Louis Philippe daybed takes center stage in the nursery, where ethereal balloon shades and a bed canopy in linen, as well as neutral upholstery and a collection of cute stuffed animals, maintain an atmosphere that's light and relaxed.

How do you combine disparate eras and styles so they feel cohesive? Look for patterns and themes that they have in common and try to connect the dots. This is easier than it sounds when you consider that many styles over history have influenced each other.

Lake House Living

You know the real estate mantra: location, location, location. Well, this lake house really has it: It's situated on top of a hill surrounded by woods on three sides and water on the other. The foyer commands a view into the trees, green and beautiful, and then spills onto the lake sparkling just beyond. It feels so serene and peaceful.

I walked in the first time and immediately fell in love.

The only problem was that the house itself didn't seem to know where it was. Because, despite the amazing locale—and active, professional, and philanthropic owners who love both natural light and the outdoors—the interiors were heavy, with hefty bones. Seemingly everything was brown: earth-tone plaster walls, wood bookcases, floors, moldings, and beams, and ponderous, traditional-style reproduction furniture that was weighing the whole place down. The scheme was muddying that treasure trove of verdure and natural light.

When you're plotting out interiors, you can gain a lot of inspiration from the world right outside the front door. So I made the lake my muse. There's a design cliché that antiques must be substantial and leaden, but I set out to prove that the opposite can be true, using pieces with elegant, slender profiles and pale, authentic finishes to elevate the mood and establish a connection to the luminous locale that would feel light as air.

First I needed the right framework, so I chose a matte shade of white paint for the walls. It's a wonderful, ethereal backdrop for Swedish eighteenth-century pieces because it references their chalky original finishes and against it, they glow. And Swedish pieces are perfect for bringing light into a room—it's actually why the Swedes painted them in the first place, to brighten Nordic winters. Using painted finishes and graceful silhouettes as common denominators, we then mixed in antiques in a similar vein from other countries to reflect my client's worldly viewpoint, along with vintage and modern furnishings and contemporary art to reflect their modern perspective.

OPPOSITE AND PRECEDING PAGE: The Swedish secretary was chosen for its sky-like, gray-blue finish and is a counterpoint to a Richard Serra print; the vintage midcentury German desk lamp and an eighteenth-century Italian candelabra both use tone and texture— a black shade much like the one in the print, chipping gilt like the secretary's chipping paint—to help bridge eras. The contemporary bench from Holly Hunt has a just-right scale for the secretary and echoes a vintage Arne Norrell chaise elsewhere in the space.

A built-in nook in the foyer is a cozy place to read a book; simple drawer pulls recall the hardware on the interior of the Swedish clock secretary in the same space. The painted Louis XV–style tables are French and play well with the Venetian palace chairs.

In the foyer, the finish on a Swedish eighteenth-century secretary with a built-in clock echoes the tones in the stone floors; nineteenth-century Swedish barrel-back chairs and eighteenth-century Venetian armchairs, all with their original finishes, command separate seating areas. Dramatic floor-to-ceiling windows, left bare to minimize the fuss, flood the space with light and lake views and let the antiques hold court.

We anchored the foyer with beautiful nineteenth-century Swedish neoclassical chairs and a Swedish secretary that all retained their original finish. Eighteenth-century painted Venetian palace chairs with sinuous silhouettes act as a glamorous counterpoint to the more restrained Nordic pieces and further uplift the space. Don't ever be afraid to skip curtains, especially if there are no neighbors in sight: We left the nearly floor-to-ceiling windows in the room bare and avoided any other distractions so as to set the furniture off and let it breathe—like carefully placed sculpture.

In the dining room, painted Swedish rococo chairs cut the severity of brown wood floors with their curvy, bright profiles. Tall and slender reproduction Knole sofas in the living room, along with a nineteenth-century Restauration mirror, accentuate the lofty height of the ceilings. The "jewelry" in the room is another eighteenth-century Swedish secretary—its faded gray-blue hue echoes the tones of the landscape just outside the window—capped by a Richard Serra print that energizes the space with a cross-cultural, century-spanning juxtaposition that could also embody the spirit of my clients. We're using objects to embody a tranquil, unexpected kind of minimalism they both love. And isn't loving what you choose to live with the whole point?

A close-up of the Swedish secretary shows how layers of paint have been painted on over centuries: a salmon wash over original pine (the plain wood is visible on the finials in the center) was later covered in cream paint. The artwork on the left that looks like a miniature landscape is actually just a carefully cut and cropped piece of finely grained stone by a Parisian artist.

A large living room with lofty ceilings calls for substantial furnishings that don't feel heavy. The scale of the reproduction Knole sofas, nineteenth-century mirror, and eighteenth-century Italian candlesticks, all with tall proportions, accentuate grand heights. Vintage midcentury campaign chairs and a contemporary cocktail table with Louis XVI-esque lines were added to give an au courant edge. Accessories include a nineteenth-century Swedish girandole and an of-the-moment resin bowl by Martha Sturdy.

ABOVE: Vintage leather sling-back campaign chairs in the living room were chosen to add interest—note their faux bamboo legs and brass finials—and comfort. **OPPOSITE**: A work by Steven Seinberg shares space with eighteenth-century Italian candlesticks—their tole tops echo tones in the painting. The contemporary console and sconces from Holly Hunt act as clean-lined frames for the vignette, which is softened by the vintage, leather-covered box on the console's lower shelf.

A sophisticated room will have layers of influence: eighteenth-century French or Swedish chairs with contemporary consoles and cocktail tables; painted Italian candelabra and midcentury modern lamps.

In the dining room, Swedish rococo chairs mingle around a Rose Tarlow Melrose House polished walnut table and act as a foil to the nineteenth-century Dutch linen press where the client stores silver and a collection of McCarty pottery. An Italian chandelier with a dramatic scale draws attention and echoes the curves in the chairs.

FINISH FIRST

Original, authentic finishes are the whole reason I take the trouble to wake up at the crack of dawn to trade with dealers while on shopping trips in Europe (the early bird truly does get the worm) and, barring rare exceptions, they're a requisite for an object to gain entry into my shipping container. Here's why: That kind of patina—the layers and layers of detail that show a chair or cabinet or secretary has been used for centuries—simply can't be replicated. Some people might call it wear and tear. I call it beautiful.

Think of a space in which everything is pristine. It makes you afraid to touch anything, set your drink down, or put your feet up. An authentic finish actually has a very meaningful design application. Nothing relaxes a room like a perfectly imperfect finish. The spot where the gilt has worn away on the arm of an eighteenth-century chair where people have rested their hands for hundreds of years is basically whispering: *Yes, I might look precious, but I'm welcoming—so have a seat.* A well-used finish invites you in and puts everything else in a room at ease.

A finish doesn't have to be centuries old to have that effect, either. In the lake house, we found a midcentury chaise and ottoman by Swedish designer Arne Norrell with a steel frame and legs that were not in perfect condition—but I didn't re-chrome them. The dull patches echo the chipped and scraped Gustavian pieces elsewhere in the house. Since the furnishings are from the same country but wildly different eras, it's as if a grandmother is chatting with her great-grandson across time. You just can't fake that kind of depth and dimension.

What to look for: With a painted piece, especially Swedish, you want to see layers. Furniture would have been passed down from generation to generation, and each would have put their own spin on a piece, splashing on gray paint over cream, salmon over blue. Gilded pieces will have what we call "scattered losses"—places where the gold has chipped away. You want to see the original wood peeking through in patches. Obviously something could have been scraped back yesterday, but if enough other signs of authenticity are present—worn areas on spots that would see use, original hardware, etc., rest assured. It should feel like there's nothing new about it.

TOP, LEFT TO RIGHT: A Régence armchair with original gilding; a nineteenth-century Empire-style tray with original black paint and gilt edges holds accessories; a vintage midcentury Arne Norrell chaise. MIDDLE, LEFT TO RIGHT: Italian altar sticks with chipping paint were repurposed into stands for European nautilus shells and pair well with a Julie Silvers bowl; a detail of a Gustavian bench shows specks of original pine. BOTTOM, LEFT TO RIGHT: A gilded nineteenth-century mirror and eighteenth-century Italian candlesticks; original hardware on a Gustavian secretary; an eighteenth-century Italian candelabra base with vintage gilded metal branches.

ABOVE: Plush velvet fabric on eighteenth-century Swedish stools is an opposites-attract pairing for a chipped and fading original finish and recalls the tone of stone floors in the entry hall, a color that's threaded throughout the house. **OPPOSITE**: In the breakfast room alone, four cultures and eras coexist— a nineteenth-century farm table with Louis XV lines, slipcovered contemporary armchairs, an eighteenth-century Venetian *canapé*, and the Gustavian stools. Since they all share undulating proportions—on arms, legs, and backs—they're harmonious and compose a more interesting arrangement than a suite of matching pieces. The artworks are by William Baggett. **FOLLOWING PAGES**: A nineteenth-century chess table boasts beautiful star marquetry. Accessories include a nineteenth-century neoclassical urn, a Wedgwood basalt footed bowl, and a midcentury globe and mortar and pestle. Louis XIV-style chairs have the presence and scale to anchor a section of the room and are quite comfortable.

SHAPE UP

To build a truly worldly perspective in an interior, you need more than one style. Fill a house with antiques from only one era and country and you might feel like you've moved into the set of *Dangerous Liaisons*—beautiful for sure, but frozen in amber and not necessarily practical for life on a planet that is increasingly connected, cross-cultural, and growing smaller every day. A sophisticated room will have layers of influence: eighteenth-century French or Swedish chairs alongside contemporary consoles and cocktail tables; painted Italian candelabra and midcentury modern lamps.

But how do you combine disparate eras and styles so they feel cohesive? Look for patterns and themes that they have in common and try to connect the dots. This is easier than it sounds when you consider that many styles over history have influenced each other: Swedish Gustavian furniture is just a Nordic version of Louis XVI; Italian artisans readily adopted the rococo lines of Louis XV.

The grid on the right depicts a selection of seating from different cultures and time periods that nevertheless live peacefully—and beautifully—in the lake house. See how the walnut frame in the Louis XIV–style chair (*top right*) mirrors that of the eighteenth-century Venetian *canapé* (*bottom left*)? Likewise, I chose the unusual painted, neoclassically inflected nineteenth-century Italian chair (*center left*) because it worked so well with the nineteenth-century Swedish barrel-back chair pictured directly above it (*top left*). See how the seat backs seem to be simpatico? The gilded Régence armchair (*center middle*) and the eighteenth-century Venetian palace chair (*bottom right*) could be cousins dressed up for the same ball. Indeed, you could probably think about mixing styles the way you mix people at a dinner party: seating together people you know will get along famously once you've had the chance to introduce them to each other.

TOP, LEFT TO RIGHT: Nineteenth-century Swedish barrel-back chair, Gustavian sofa bench, Louis XIV–style chair. MIDDLE, LEFT TO RIGHT: Nineteenth-century Italian chair, giltwood Régence armchair, vintage midcentury campaign chair. BOTTOM, LEFT TO RIGHT: Venetian *canapé*, Swedish chair, Venetian palace chair, all eighteenth century.

A Directoire settee with details in an original black finish is a focal point in the master bedroom and is paired with contemporary armchairs that boast similarly clean lines. The still life of shellfish is by Belgian artist Jules Brouwers.

ABOVE: A pair of eighteenth-century forged iron candlesticks have scrolling bases that mirror each other but are inverted—an original flourish by the artisan that charmed the homeowners; a vintage champagne bucket holds moss. OPPOSITE: A Spanish occasional table, nailhead covered box, vintage vellum-covered books, and English stool with its original leather are pretty and functional, offering both a surface to set down a cup of coffee and a place to hide the remote.

The transitional, Louis XIV–era commodes are
a brother-and-sister pair (alike but not strictly
matching) that flank the contemporary hand-
forged iron bed. The silver-gilt Louis Philippe
mirror helps cement a silver-blue color scheme
and makes the most of tall ceilings. The eighteenth-
century Italian silver-gilt bench wears a leopard
print—a subdued pop of pattern in the room.

ABOVE: A console made from a salvaged European balcony, Greek and Belgian jardinières, and a nineteenth-century Italian candelabra create an evocative outdoor dining area.
OPPOSITE: A vintage stone table with a marble top captures the tone of the stone floors in the foyer—marking a clear connection between indoors and out.

As delectable as Victorian houses may look from the outside, they *can* sometimes be complex indoors. The challenge lies in creating fluid, functional spaces that feel vibrant and complement the house's original allure.

Let Architecture Lead the Way

To paraphrase a famous saying, when it comes to interior design, architecture is destiny. It leads the way in all decisions, and any scheme you devise should feel harmonious with the house itself. This can be an advantage when working from the ground up, but it can also be a challenge, especially when dealing with a historic structure designed in a time when lifestyles were different—which leads us to this charming Victorian.

The homeowners, a young career couple involved in one of the city's sports teams, are avid collectors of both antiques and art, with keen eyes for distinctive pieces. They entertain often and are understandably proud of their house—just look at the wedding-cake façade of the nineteenth-century abode. Talk about curb appeal. But here's the thing about Victorians: As delectable as they may look from the outside, they *can* sometimes be complex indoors. That's because they were built when lives were more formal, with interiors often broken up into smaller spaces meant for different types of entertaining in an age when social boundaries were wrought-iron rigid.

In this case, the lower floor is divided into not one but two parlors (one once reserved for family and another once meant for company), a dining room, and a kitchen. What's more, the foyer, dining room, and kitchen are arranged shotgun-style (in one straight line), and the dining room was feeling like an afterthought—essentially a glorified hallway. These days we might organize all those rooms into one lofty, loosely connected open-plan space where lounging, dining, entertaining, and cooking mingle in one fell swoop, but we didn't have the luxury of architectural alterations. We had to figure out a way to create fluid, functional spaces that would feel as vibrant as the family and be a proper showcase for their art and antiques, all while complementing details that were part of the Victorian's original allure.

OPPOSITE: A seating arrangement in one of the parlors with a Louis XVI table and Directoire chair takes advantage of a sunny window to highlight finishes; note how the alabaster lamp catches this light with opaline radiance. The painting, in a gilt Louis XVI frame to complement the furniture, is by Hunt Slonem and is indicative of the homeowners' taste for vibrant contemporary art. PRECEDING PAGES: This stately Victorian is located in the lower Garden District of New Orleans.

Covering millwork in the foyer with a luminous white paint helps put the spotlight on the kind of craftsmanship that's a real boon in historic houses like this Victorian and lightens the scheme to boot. The glass-fronted door and transom with swirling mullions recalls a wave motif on the exterior wood siding.

ABOVE: The foyer is arranged shotgun-style with the dining room and kitchen, in a straight line from the front to the back of the house. To prevent the dining room from feeling like a mere walk-through, a grisaille mural wallpaper was installed to give it an alluring personality that softly draws you in. A large-scale contemporary still life, along with unusual, eighteenth-century Louis XIV-style painted Italian chairs, a nineteenth-century Italian chandelier, and a contemporary console and lamps, make the foyer feel substantial and create a fresh, youthful introduction to the Victorian residence; entryways are important first impressions and should give hints of what's to come. OPPOSITE: In one of the parlors, an eighteenth-century gilt Italian console accentuates colorful paintings by Clementine Hunter, while a nineteenth-century French terra-cotta garden urn grounds the arrangement. PRECEDING PAGES: An eighteenth-century Swedish secretary and vintage Savonarola chair make a stair landing functional for storage and correspondence. A seventeenth-century East Asian vase holds tulips.

If you want instant drama in a dining room, opt for a mural wallpaper. A scenic grisaille—a design rendered entirely in tones of gray—from French purveyor Zuber made the space singular in its own right, quietly drawing you in from the foyer, where vibrant art sets a strong tone as you walk in the house. To unify the parlors, which are divided by pocket doors, we covered original millwork-like cove ceilings in a custom white lacquer from Fine Paints of Europe that's seductive and dramatic, ideal for entertaining. (Even if you're painting a space white, investing in a top-shelf brand does make a difference, giving you a powerful foundation for the rest of the design.) Seating arrangements are organized in inviting groups that weave the rooms together, great for having a friend or two over for coffee or for groups of guests at a party. The art and antiques are the real icing on this particular cake, with unexpected juxtapositions of furniture, paintings, and sculpture creating a final flourish.

A whale vertebra on a stand is a tactile counterpoint to a vase by Kelly Wearstler and a horn bowl.

ABOVE: The rough-hewn contours of a contemporary Julie Silvers female sculpture is a fine match for a nineteenth-century Louis XVI–style table with a worn finish. OPPOSITE: A Louis XV commode with its original hardware and an eighteenth-century Italian candelabra come from the same style era—obvious in their curling proportions—so they are a natural pairing.

The main statement in the dining room is the grisaille mural wallpaper by Zuber, which transformed it from a mere walk-through space into a destination in its own right—complete with a view. The only other flourishes are eighteenth-century Italian Directoire-style dining chairs covered in a fluffy, curly hide. The mingling of other casual and refined touches—a painted Louis XV *enfilade*, Louis XIV chairs with their original leather upholstery, a Murano chandelier, and Julie Silvers ceramic vessels— creates a relaxed aesthetic.

We had to figure out a way to create fluid, functional spaces that would feel as vibrant as the family and be a proper showcase for their art.

When they entertain, the clients foster a happy sense of occasion and use items from their wide-ranging antiques collection, like this vintage silver-plated meat trolley, which they really do roll out for dinner parties. The nineteenth-century English buffet holds china and is topped with nineteenth-century giltwood Italian architectural fragments on stands.

A pair of Louis XVI marquis and a Louis XIV buffet inspired a sophisticated color scheme, with the blue-gray of their finishes used to contrast the sleek ebonized wood of the piano and black leather on midcentury Maison Jansen chairs. The idiosyncratic Napoleon III *rafraîchissoir* is a nineteenth-century French wine cooler. The eighteenth-century Genoese chandelier layers in more glamour, while Missoni pillows on the chairs give them a contemporary edge.

A Marriage of Art and Antiques

One of the biggest thrills I get out of working with antiques is putting them together with contemporary art. There's just something about the combination of those two disciplines—a functional piece made by hand by someone in another time and an artistic expression carefully wrought to convey something meaningful about our current age—that electrifies a room like nothing else can. Combined, they create an artistic statement all their own, one that hopefully says something about the homeowners themselves, as individual as a signature or a fingerprint.

There are no hard-and-fast rules, but to get the mix right, use shape, color, and texture as a loose guide. You might even think of yourself as a matchmaker, introducing items that have things in common.

In this parlor I had a great jumping-off point with a painting by artist Hunt Slonem, one of two the clients owned. It's lush with vivid hues and florid brushstrokes, features the silhouettes of rabbits—a recurring theme in Slonem's work—and is housed in an equally impressive eighteenth-century Louis XV frame with its original gilding. The pointed bunny ears in the painting as well as the gilt frame immediately made me think of a piece I'd seen by

David Borgerding, a sculptor who makes elegant abstract sculptures in brushed and painted metal. The work is a clustered bouquet of curving shapes with two points that jut out just like the ears in the painting. What's more, it had a gold finish (a nod to the gilding) that purposely shows Borgerding's brushstrokes (a nod to the painting). Placing the two together over the mantel gave the room an exciting thrum we all loved.

Across the room we wanted to place a larger-scale sculpture by artist Julie Silvers, a haunting primitivist-esque composition made of clay that almost looks like a cairn of stacked stones. To counter its rough-hewn nature—opposites do, after all, attract—I put it on a wooden plinth, an elegant neoclassical platform that gives it height. Nearby, vintage Maison Jansen sling chairs in black leather pick up the color of the sculpture to ground it more fully in the room, but the pièces de résistance were two nineteenth-century Italian fragments sprouting fleur-de-lis-like fronds that were mounted in the windows. Their tall, elongated proportions mimic the sculpture's, but in elegant painted wood and gilt edging—a yin-yang match and unexpected flourish for ordinary windows.

TOP, LEFT TO RIGHT: A painting by Hunt Slonem in an eighteenth-century Louis XV gilt frame and a sculpture by David Borgerding have enough in common to create an engaging arrangement, even though they seem unrelated in theme and approach. BOTTOM, LEFT TO RIGHT: Vintage Maison Jansen slingback chairs and nineteenth-century Italian fragments mounted in the window help to accentuate a sculpture by Julie Silvers on a plinth.

The clean-lined kitchen gains warmth from a simple Louis XV-inflected hood and stone floors. The vintage mouchoir jardinières—so named because they resemble bunched-up handkerchiefs—by Willy Guhl are used as countertop accessories to help bridge the space to the back garden, visible through windows and doors.

A corona hung with Italian polished cotton curtains distinguishes the mostly monochromatic and serene master bedroom, which wouldn't have the same drama without it; a vintage Louis XV-style chandelier and a B.Viz bolster pillow made from an antique tapestry pick up the Louis XV theme. The bench covered in a zebra print wears the only other pattern, and a gilt rococo mirror with original glass is the only other statement. To conform to the palette, a headboard the client already owned was painted in a creamy lacquer.

ABOVE: An Italian eighteenth-century gilt console is an unconventional bedside table, whose tones are reprised in a contemporary urn and mounted nineteenth-century Italian decorative fragment. **OPPOSITE**: A sharply proportioned contemporary console allows the gilt rococo mirror to garner all the attention.

Contemporary and vintage furnishings like a canopy bed, Eames-style chair and ottoman, and bamboo blinds are fresh and age-appropriate for the son's room; a nineteenth-century chandelier, European family crest, and eighteenth-century Italian reclining chair give the space context so it feels cohesive with the rest of the house. Hand-carved footed stools are based on seventeenth-century originals and are covered in an alpaca bouclé to counterbalance the sleekness of the canopy bed. The *bibliothèque* is an idiosyncratic storage piece that displays antique vellum books and has doors to hide clothing, sports gear, and electronics.

The design of this house, with its surrounding gardens, blurs the lines between outside and in. It's a sublime way to live.

Bringing the Outside In

Picture a house surrounded by lush gardens: olive trees, Savannah hollies, boxwood parterres, gravel-covered terraces, and multiple fountains, so the sound of running water is never far away. Nine months out of the year, doors are flung open to the breeze, traffic flows freely between indoor and outdoor dining rooms and kitchens, and with gurgling water and the crunch of gravel under feet, you feel thousands of miles away—Provence, Tuscany, Umbria—not the middle of a modern American city.

It's a sublime way to live and no accident that this house was built around the exterior features with the intent of blurring the boundaries between outside and in—just like they do in France. When they approached me for an interior refresh, they wanted to up the ante style-wise and further blur those boundaries, using antiques as stepping-stones. You don't always have to start from scratch. Sometimes, to breathe new life into interiors that you have loved and enjoyed for years, all you need to do is recognize your most treasured pieces, move them forward, and build around them with significant statement pieces or furnishings with integrity.

A couple of memorable pieces that were already in place provided our biggest new brushstrokes: two beautiful, large-scale ecclesiastical paintings, probably once altarpieces, that had been hiding at the top of the stairs. It's a good lesson—sometimes moving something you already love to a new location will give it and its environment a whole new life. I brought the paintings down to the living room and put them front and center, then calibrated everything else so they'd get the attention they deserve. They're striking, especially when paired with low-slung contemporary sofas and tables and a massive Louis XIV armoire in a whisper-soft shade of weathered oak.

OPPOSITE: In the living room, where two massive nineteenth-century ecclesiastical paintings by Victor Mazies are the major focal point, furnishings went mostly in the other direction to create the of-the-moment balance the homeowners craved, including a contemporary chair with an enveloping, alpaca-covered cushion, a luxe hit of texture. **PRECEDING PAGES:** The wrought-iron balustrade in the foyer inspired a seating arrangement centered on a rattan chair (the iron base reprises the staircase material) that also embodies the house's indoor-outdoor aesthetic. A seventeenth-century frame highlights a work by the daughter of the family, a clever technique that elevates a memento into a statement suffused with meaning. The eighteenth-century Italian console holds an antique Tibetan dowry box. The cowhide rug helps define the space and gently deepens the monochromatic palette. **FOLLOWING PAGES:** To give the paintings all the attention, other furnishings are low-slung and include a mix of contemporary and antique pieces—a Christian Liaigre sofa, a Jiun Ho bronze table, and an eighteenth-century Gustavian daybed—and all upholstery is neutral, a unifying technique that allows pieces from different eras to happily coexist.

To pull the open-air attitude indoors, we whittled down an existing collection of French Provençal furniture—it was reading too brown and heavy for the vibe we were looking for—and brought in a few star outdoor pieces that better suited the atmosphere. Garden antiques, especially those boasting plenty of patina, can make great indoor furnishings because they tend to have an important, monumental scale (since they were used in open spaces) and an exposed-to-the-elements sensibility that's a tonic inside a home. In the foyer, a contemporary chair woven from rattan—a material typical of outdoor furniture—mingles with art and an eighteenth-century Italian console to set the mood. A console table composed of two eighteenth-century sandstone plinths topped with a beautifully waxed nineteenth-century walnut plateau sits behind the sofa in the living room and adds earthy, under-the-radar texture. The dining room table is made from weathered exterior architectural fragments topped with a clean, white slab of marble—rough-hewn and refined all at once.

Of course, all of that handiwork would be for naught if the garden itself weren't as inviting as the interiors. Furnish outdoor rooms the way you would those indoors and you can't go wrong. Under a wisteria arbor, the vintage outdoor dining table boasts a marble top, the iron chandelier illuminates evenings with candlelight, and antique garden chairs are covered with ample cushions, so guests can linger for hours (page 193).

OPPOSITE AND PRECEDING PAGES: The console table, made from eighteenth-century sandstone garden plinths and a nineteenth-century walnut plateau, was cut so it would be two inches shorter than the back of the sofa. Varying furniture heights like this—the same is true for the Louis XIV armoire and Gustavian daybed, as well as the sofa and cocktail and end tables—creates a layered effect that's pleasing to look at and gives the impression that pieces were accumulated over time.

Garden antiques, especially those boasting plenty of patina, can make great indoor furnishings because they tend to have an important, monumental scale and an exposed-to-the-elements sensibility that's a tonic inside a home.

When it comes to statement lighting, opt for something you'd want to look at for the rest of your life—not a guarantee with a contemporary or even a vintage piece, but a fair assumption with an eighteenth-century Genoese model that's already stood the test of time. The art is by Lynn Sanders.

The dining table, made from vintage architectural fragments, had a Belgian bluestone top, but a dark stone like that would have felt leaden in the luminous space; a new marble slab gives the table a sleek edge. To take advantage of pool views and dissolve lines between indoors and out, windows were left bare. Contemporary chairs reprise tones in a nineteenth-century ebonized *enfilade*, or buffet. The stool is African.

ABOVE: An Italian mirror composed of eighteenth- and nineteenth-century fragments reflects the color of one of the paintings, unobtrusively creating another piece of "art" that doesn't compete for the spotlight; the eighteenth-century bench is Swedish.
OPPOSITE: The Gustavian clock secretary brings another elevation into the room and has cabinets beneath the desktop that double as storage.

ABOVE AND OPPOSITE: Diverse furnishings and accessories like an eighteenth-century Italian candelabra, vintage urn, ecclesiastical statue, vintage table base, and nineteenth-century Venetian mirror feel of a piece thanks to patina. **PRECEDING PAGES**: In the master bedroom, the headboard was shortened to give it a livable scale, though it still retains a hefty presence that's highlighted by a nineteenth-century Venetian mirror. The Empire armchair and ottoman is the kind of distinct piece a collector can keep for a lifetime, reupholstering the duo to make it relevant for new settings. The nineteenth-century commodes are French, the eighteenth-century bench is Swedish, and the eighteenth- to nineteenth-century chandelier is Italian, as are the contemporary photographs.

RIGHT: As a major bridge to the outdoor spaces—the exterior kitchen and dining area are just outside those doors—the kitchen adopts many touches reminiscent of the outdoors like terra-cotta floors (typical of Italy or the South of France), fittings that look like garden spouts, and tole lanterns. FOLLOWING PAGES: The outdoor dining area is an inviting oasis, furnished like a room that happens to have a wisteria arbor for a ceiling, with vintage tables and chairs, an iron chandelier, and gravel underfoot, which is so much more evocative than stone pavers. An antique fountain that probably once stood in a town square and pool views make for transporting outdoor meals.

MAKE EVERY DAY A HOLIDAY

These homeowners are devotees of the South of France, and there are reminders of it all over the house as well as in their verdant garden. But it's especially present in the way they entertain. In New Orleans, the weather is mild for much of the year, which means they pull the feast outdoors and use fresh air, flowing water, and lush greenery to curate the kind of atmosphere that completely sweeps guests away. If you're lucky enough to live in a temperate area of the country, think about your exterior spaces with this in mind, particularly when it comes to dining, because a meal in the open air changes the entire equation.

Mimic the standard dining room formula—table, chairs, lighting—with weather-resistant furnishings and get creative in how you deploy them. Vintage wrought-iron furniture is a classic that will stand the test of time (pluses if it's slightly rusty and has chipping paint), but wicker and teak can also weather beautifully. And don't underestimate the transformative power of a chandelier—I've seen evocative versions hung from tree branches—to provide an instant sense of occasion. You don't need acres of plots overflowing with blooms,

either. The only things a small patio or even city terrace needs to transform it into an enchanted garden are plants potted in jardinières or terra-cotta pots. See how it changes the way you feel about your morning cup of coffee—it makes an ordinary Wednesday feel like a mini vacation.

If you don't live in an area of the country that lets you take advantage of Mother Nature aside from during the summer months, you can still get that million-miles-away feeling during the other seasons from kitchen and dining accessories imbued with the same romance. These clients have built up an impressive collection of such "smalls": silver flatware, French and Italian confit and confiture crocks, wonderfully carved vintage and antique cutting boards, classic copper pots. They display much of them on open shelves in the kitchen, but the pieces would look just as good hanging on a wall or clustered together at the end of a counter or in the center of the table. Then pull them out for parties—fill crocks or pots with flowers or herbs, use cutting boards to serve bread or crackers and cheese, mix and match different patterns of flatware. *Trop charmant!*

Moving the party outdoors makes entertaining effervescent, and evocative decorative accessories can do double duty as serving pieces to provide some of the atmosphere if plein air meals are not an option, including vintage silver, cutting boards, copper pots, and confit and confiture crocks.

A minimalist interior can be an especially dramatic backdrop in which to showcase storied pieces and really let them shine.

Antiques in a Modern World

What happens when your clients are attracted to the cutting edge but also harbor a passion for centuries-old objects? The seemingly incompatible attractions can actually lay the groundwork for a harmonious union. In fact, a minimalist interior can be an especially dramatic backdrop in which to showcase storied pieces—precisely my MO in a new condominium I designed for a young family in a converted school.

The husband, a young entrepreneur in the movie business, was a second-generation client who grew up in an antiques-filled home I'd curated for his parents. He and his wife had an appreciation for the depth such pieces can bring to an interior, but as go-getters in an of-the-moment industry, they wanted their home to reflect their fresh, finger-on-the-pulse perspective.

For the right effect within such parameters, fine-tune the backdrop first. Ebonized floors in a spectacularly glossy sheen and white walls in a matte, plaster-y finish established a frill-free, operatic setting that would highlight distinctive finds but was also tactile. To delineate the living area from the dining room and kitchen (one wide, open-plan space), we added a fireplace and had a decorative painter cover it in Venetian plaster to add even more texture. Into that sharply edited environment, we composed arrangements that straddled eras and aesthetics.

When you pare down a space, everything you *do* keep stands out more. Be keen on quality and character. Case in point: a show-stopping pair of rare, eighteenth-century Venetian rococo chairs with silver gilt that hold court in this living room like sculpture. Elsewhere, we designed an entire powder room around an eighteenth-century Venetian rococo mirror with gilt scrolls. In the master bedroom, an eighteenth-century Flemish tapestry and a midcentury black-and-gilt Venetian bombé chest have starring roles in a sea of subdued ivory and cream.

To balance all that personality, new furnishings complement the antiques while also imprinting their own subtle stamp on the space. A contemporary French sofa in the living room is covered in a linen that echoes the finish on the rococo chairs. In the powder room, sconces made from onyx slices glow with a richness that recalls the gilt on the mirror. A curvaceous bed in the master bedroom sets off the tapestry with a sinuous suggestion of movement. Pulling it all together is an abundance of natural light and lots of space between arrangements so they have plenty of room to breathe.

OPPOSITE: A pair of rare eighteenth-century Venetian rococo chairs, showing bits of their original silver gilt and the gesso underneath, have enough personality to form the centerpiece of a modernist living room arrangement in which all the other elements strike a softer note. PRECEDING SPREAD: Contemporary elements like an acrylic occasional table, cocktail table, and low-slung French sofa help set off the antiques while keeping the vibe current; midcentury Venetian mirrors prevent a swathe of white space from getting too spare. OPENING PAGE: Theatrical, high-gloss black floors set the stage for an electric pairing of the old and new. A nineteenth-century Greek jardinière echoes the silhouette of a contemporary chandelier and helps to ground all the sheen from the floors.

ABOVE: In a wide, open-plan space that also includes a dining area and the kitchen, a floor-to-ceiling fireplace, equipped with a ventless gas hearth, was installed to delineate the living room; its Venetian plaster finish warms up the space with color and texture, bridges high-gloss floors to matte white walls, and references the finish on antique Venetian chairs. OPPOSITE: Powdery white walls make an eighteenth-century Swedish barrel-back chair with its original paint feel right at home. Using accessories that all have gold-toned accents—a vintage brass telescope, a gilt eighteenth-century crown, midcentury Venetian mirrors, and eighteenth-century altar sticks—is a way to unify objects with wildly different backgrounds. The painting is by Steven Seinberg.

When you pare down
a space, everything
you *do* keep stands out
more. Be keen on
quality and character.

In the dining area, Louis XVI-style chairs were covered in patent leather, which mirror high-gloss floors in a practical, wipe-clean material. The nineteenth-century Empire-style chandelier has adaptable and clean lines—making it a good choice in sleek settings—and tall proportions that help anchor the contemporary table without blocking views through to the living room.

Restricting the finishes in
the kitchen to rich wood or
matte white tones makes sleek
built-in architecture and the
latest appliances hospitable to
antiques and keeps to the
overall interior color scheme.

ABOVE: A graphic wallpaper by Kelly Wearstler gives a built-in bar area personality, but since it's in a subdued black-and-white colorway, it won't overpower any other element in a wide-open space. **OPPOSITE**: A Louis Philippe commode makes an awkward niche between the living room and kitchen functional, providing storage for a collection of vintage silver; adding a mirror such as a nineteenth-century neoclassical trumeau is like creating an interior window. **FOLLOWING PAGES**: A modern residence incorporates the unexpected, including an Empire Italian bookcase, vintage French silver and Italian porcelain, a nineteenth-century Empire-style Italian chandelier with lithe lines, nineteenth-century decanters and porcelain, intricate marquetry, and a collection of vintage and antique silver flatware.

MATERIAL WORLD

Simplicity is deceptive. On the surface, the materials and finishes on the walls, floors, and architectural features of this project seem to dissolve into the background, but they are actually some of its most important features, speaking volumes, albeit in a whisper. Since we wanted to give the antiques in this residence a modern sensibility, the bones of the place needed to establish that aesthetic. But I had to tread carefully, choosing minimalist elements that would connect to those objects and feel warm enough in a home for a young family.

To do this you have to think about tone and texture. Ebonized floors polished to a high sheen gave me a seductive stage that had a suitably glamorous edge. To counter that slickness, however, I needed walls that would read soft. For those we used Benjamin Moore's matte Aura paint in White Dove, a fabulous product that is so tactile it attains the illusion of plaster (which also tempers the high-wattage effect of its stark hue, chosen for the way it reflected the prodigious natural light).

The "bridge" between the walls and the floors became a soaring fireplace in which we installed a ventless, gas-burning hearth. I commissioned a decorative painter to layer it with black Venetian plaster, a technique where powdered minerals like marble are mixed into the compound to give it incredible dimension, in this case showing misty gray tonal variations that referenced the floors, the steel of the hearth, and the walls all at once. The treatment is distinctive enough that it actually became a focal point (on which there was no need to hang any art) and warmed the room by several degrees—a result you could not have gotten with plain Sheetrock.

From there, it was a short leap to the antiques, returning to tone and texture as the threads to connect it all. In the living room, the gorgeously weathered finishes on the eighteenth-century Venetian rococo chairs and a Swedish barrel-back chair have an elegant rapport with the textured walls and Venetian plaster. I covered Louis XVI–style chairs in the dining area in patent leather, a practical nod to the shiny floors.

In a stairwell connecting public and private areas, walls were painted in a high-gloss lacquer to elevate a space that's normally an afterthought. The color matches the tone of linen upholstery on the living room sofa to weave both spaces together. Flashes of gold and brass—on the eighteenth-century Swedish clock and Italian chandelier, custom mirror, and stair rail—give the passageway even more cohesion.

RIGHT: Because the eighteenth-century Flemish tapestry makes such a statement in the master bedroom, everything else was edited down to shapes and textures, including an elegant sleigh-like bed in ivory linen (which seems to point towards the wall hanging), lamps made from salvaged balustrades, low contemporary bedside tables, and eighteenth-century Swedish stools. FOLLOWING PAGES: An eighteenth-century rococo Venetian mirror dominates the powder room, but contemporary onyx sconces (that play up the mirror's finish) energize the composition with a modern-day appeal. That interplay also holds true in the master bathroom, where a rare eighteenth-century French mirror is a foil for a sleek bathtub.

LIVE YOUR LIFE

I have this conversation with clients all the time: They adore antiques, but they're afraid of using seemingly precious objects in everyday settings—home offices, kitchens, dining rooms—where they'll be subjected to the wear and tear of life. *How can I justify using a piece of furniture that may be the last of its kind,* the reasoning goes, *in a place where it might get banged, bruised, scratched, or otherwise abused?*

What I love about using antiques is that generations before us have made wonderful memories with them, imparting dents and dings that add to their story. If a piece has lasted this long, there's nothing your children or pets can do to it that's going to be worse than three hundred years of use. And your own dings and dents are only going to improve its appeal. What's more, choosing things with well-worn patinas (meaning they already *have* dings) gives you the freedom to use them in high-traffic areas because they're already imperfect.

When I started working with these clients, they had one child (they now have three!), so there was no room for pieces that were so precious you couldn't touch them. Tables and chests on which the original finish has long since worn off are perfect for this. I didn't refinish the Louis Philippe commode in their dining area or the eighteenth-century bed or Provençal sideboard in their guest room for precisely that reason. (Full disclosure: I rarely, if ever, refinish furniture pieces—and truth be told, a piece with a pristine finish isn't going to make it into my shipping container, either.)

A unique piece of furniture also has a way of making chores feel special. When I'm shopping in Europe, I'm looking for the kind of tables, chairs, and secretaries that will make your friends and family do a double take and say: *Wow! You pay bills in that chair?* That was my line of thinking when I found these clients a highly unusual midcentury modern chair for their home office. It has an elegant, sculptural seat the likes of which I'd never seen—a marriage of beauty and function that I think rises to the level of art, but is perfectly compatible with answering emails.

A midcentury modern Italian chair makes this home office with built-in cabinetry feel alive and impressive; it lures the user into daily tasks like fielding emails or paying bills.

An eighteenth-century transitional Louis XV-XVI bed in French oak that has never been refinished is perfect for a casual home because it has a weathered and welcoming feel; the table is an eighteenth-century Italian piece.

ABOVE: A vintage French neoclassical demilune table with an unusual stretcher holds quartz, tulips, and eighteenth-century Italian candlesticks. The art is actually a framed intaglio from my licensed RH line.
OPPOSITE: A midcentury black-and-gilt Venetian bombé commode in the master bedroom would really be over-the-top if it weren't for the stark and serene surroundings. A bronze midcentury French urn and contemporary ceramics reprise the color scheme.

A 30,000-square-foot, five-bedroom home makes the best kind of canvas—an opportunity to compose a collection using storied pieces as building blocks to furnish in a distinct personality that will evolve over a lifetime.

Break the plan down and proceed room-by-room, piece-by-piece. Start with the "heroes," the memorable, worthy, and head-turning objects that strike a dramatic note, then fill in around them, complementing or contrasting against them as you go.

OPPOSITE: Bit by bit, build an atmosphere that's luxurious and distinct with objects that have character and integrity, including (from top, left to right) a neoclassical terra-cotta urn, eighteenth-century gilt Italian candlesticks, a neoclassical-style Italian daybed, a Brutalist sculpture and Gustavian buffet, eighteenth-century Italian gilt finials, a nineteenth-century Spanish table, a nineteenth-century garden urn, a Gustavian table, and a vintage ram's head mirror. FOLLOWING PAGES: The dining room is a blend of pieces from different eras and styles with tone and color in common so they feel destined for each other, like a Gustavian table and buffet, Louis XVI and contemporary Italian dining chairs, midcentury mirrors, and a console and a chandelier by Lindsey Adelman.

ABOVE: A handpainted wallpaper dominates a powder room and sticks to a black-and-white theme to help set off a nineteenth-century repoussé mirror. **OPPOSITE**: A Pedro Friedeberg hand chair is a distinctive vintage piece that acts as a hallway focal point where the only other flourishes are eighteenth-century gilt Italian mirrors and French rock crystal pendants.

To quietly distinguish the otherwise understated cooking and prep area in the kitchen, the marble backsplash was cut with a curving rococo-esque profile and a book-matched graining that matches the counters. The nineteenth-century lanterns are not an exact pair—resist the urge to make everything perfect and a space will feel relaxed. Contemporary stools are covered in leather for wipe-clean ease.

ABOVE: Vintage silver domes make elegant kitchen accessories. **OPPOSITE**: The breakfast nook table was made from a whitewashed tree trunk base and a matte zinc top and pulled up to a nine-foot, velvet-covered banquette. The contemporary Italian chairs have supple leather seats that relate to brown tones throughout the house and introduce a welcome sense of texture.

The master sitting room connects to the master bedroom and is a hangout spot for the entire family, furnished for style and comfort. **ABOVE**: A nineteenth-century, Louis XVI-style daybed and a nineteenth-century French occasional table furnish a reading nook. **OPPOSITE**: With a sleek herringbone brick hearth, the nineteenth-century marble fireplace gets a stylish update; the starburst piece is a nineteenth-century French barometer. **PRECEDING PAGES**: A large-scale eighteenth-century Italian mirror with elaborate gilt carving inspired the use of an African textile on throw pillows, which pick up a tonal detail in the mirror and translate it for a global, cross-cultural era.

RIGHT: The wife's dressing room is one of the only areas in the house to depart from the black-and-white color scheme—the soft gray tones on the wall were meant to create an enveloping effect where she could lounge with friends and family. The centerpiece of the room is a vintage pleated leather sofa whose shape is reprised in contemporary swivel chairs. The eighteenth-century Italian mirror is propped against the wall—a casual touch that's also functional for checking out shoes. FOLLOWING PAGES: Since marble side tables make such a design statement, simple floxed mirrors—mirrors composed of individual panels—were the only other flourishes needed in the master bedroom. The clients wanted a custom nine-foot-by-nine-foot bed so their children could crawl in while the parents wouldn't sacrifice any comfort—a win-win, since its large scale helps to tame a room with large proportions. The eighteenth-century Swedish bench was left with its burlap underlayer exposed, a plainspoken touch of texture that tames rarified details like quartz crystal lamps.

UNCOMMON COLOR

In my design projects and my own home, I tend to avoid overt splashes of color, preferring instead to let the painted finishes and weathered wood in the antiques I love take the main focus. But that doesn't mean I don't appreciate the nuanced way a uniform palette can provide a useful framework for all the other design choices in a house and even allow space for the occasional pop of vivid hues.

Take our use of black and white as a harmonizing theme in nearly every room of this house. As shades go, black and white are often thought of as neutral, noncolors. But use them consistently and they gain a strong personality all their own. They can bring everything in a room into crisp focus, and if you employ the right materials, can strike a yin-yang balance between the plainspoken and the sophisticated.

The ground-floor powder room is my best argument for all of the above, a bold design statement with real character, wrought almost entirely in two hues. The main element is a hand-painted, stripe-like wallpaper that runs from the floor to the ceiling. We matched the white in the pattern to the tone of white on the walls throughout the house, so the space feels connected to the larger space. The pattern itself is reminiscent of the graining in the marble vanity, even more harmony.

The wall covering has energy and movement, and feels of-the-moment, but it gets along tremendously well with the nineteenth-century French repoussé mirror. That malleability is a hallmark of a black-and-white palette and it's a real asset.

In the living room, the color combination does the exact opposite, fading into the background as a framing device that heightens all the furnishings, like eighteenth-century gilded Venetian mirrors and a bolster covered in a brightly patterned African textile. But even with exalted pieces like the Beaux Arts fireplace, the space remains casual. That's because all the black-and-white finishes are matte: the paint on the walls, the steel frames on the windows and doors, a Venetian plaster finish on the piano, the painted frame of the nineteenth-century Italian daybed, a concrete table lamp.

Of course, throughout, I also had to weave in the dusky shades of brown I adore so much in antiques with patina. In a strict black-and-white environment, they provide a necessary extra layer of dimension. I mixed tones and finishes here, too, for added depth, from the polished, book-matched walnut of the Biedermeier table in the foyer to the weathered oak of the nineteenth-century Spanish table in the living room, to the creamy leather on chairs in the breakfast nook. Luckily the black-and-white scheme can handily accommodate them all.

A crisp black-and-white color scheme gives you a strong foundation to build in pops of personality and color and set off objects and antiques; it also has a strong and sophisticated personality all its own.

A monumental French limestone park bench dominates the entry path to the mudroom with an Old World panache and patina that gives new architecture a sense of history.

Guerilla Antiquing

When I go on a buying trip, which I do about four times a year, it's a serious affair: A typical three-week itinerary would include eighteen cities and towns across Italy and France and a bevy of hotels, rental cars, trains, markets, warehouses, stalls, fairs, and dealers. That isn't to suggest that you have to dive into antiquing like it's your full-time job in order to discover something special or get a good deal, but you will benefit from adopting my flexible mind-set, even if you're only dipping your toe into the sport by spending a morning at one of the Paris *puces*.

The most important thing I would teach someone just starting to acquire is that you have to be open to possibility. It's a treasure hunt. The most thrilling thing about it is that you never know what you're going to find. You can't approach the enterprise with a single focus or a shopping list. You might go to Europe in search of a Louis XVI armoire and shop the flea markets and fairs and simply not find it. *For years.* But if you're receptive, you're going to find other treasures that you can use. Hopefully you'll also have the insight to purchase them. If you can think of the mission as fluid and ever evolving and play the long game, you will have far greater traction. Little by little, you will acquire things that speak to you and pretty soon your home will be filled with pieces that are as distinct as you are.

Don't rush it. I've had buying days where I've come up with zero and that's just part of the process. On the other hand, try to get good at recognizing the pitter-patter of your heart when you find something that really resonates with you and don't ignore that, either. Because in the case of antiques you literally might never see it again. Listening to that instinct has never once led me astray, saddled with an object I later decide I don't want. Ignoring it, however, has left me heartbroken more than once.

Lastly, don't forget that that this kind of shopping is an experience in itself. Revel in it. If you're the kind of person who's going to go to markets, fairs, and auctions in Europe, you're an adventurer. You want nice things for your home and you know that requires some effort, a little soul-searching, and broadening of your horizons. Sometimes, I'll be in the thick of it, having been on the road for days, when I find myself at one of the local brasseries in a quaint town, eating a *plat du jour* for ten euros at a sidewalk table on a sunny day, or outdoors at a *déballage,* or fair, in the countryside, sitting on a piece of used furniture in the middle of a field, enjoying the paella I just bought from a vendor. I always want to pinch myself. That kind of magical moment is the best treasure of all.

Examining a monumental gate at an *entrepôt,* or warehouse, in an area off the rue de Rosiers in Saint-Ouen, where many of the Paris flea markets are located. Be sure to wander around the streets immediately surrounding the markets; many of the vendors there specialize in garden elements and exterior furnishings.

WHAT I LOOK FOR

While I don't shop markets, fairs, and auctions with a shopping list in mind, there are a few objects, forms, and styles I'm always on the lookout for, because of how useful they are from a designer's point of view. These pieces are practical no matter what your specific needs are, and I promise you'll eventually find a good place for them. I've never had a client that couldn't benefit from more storage, whether it's a place to hide the TV and electronics in the living room or a cache to stash clothes—case goods like armoires and commodes handily fit the bill. Daybeds are my go-to for living room seating because their open sides mean they can be placed anywhere in the space without visually cluttering it up, and they tend to blend well with contemporary furniture. Stools are always a shoo-in because they provide extra seating in a dining or living room or at the foot of the bed. Statement lighting is another practical buy—a beautiful chandelier or pair of sconces can instantly make a room. Unexpected items that you can display as art—whether that's collections of cameos you frame or an architectural fragment like a shield or coat of arms you hang above the fireplace—are the kind of thing that imbue a home with instant character that can't be replicated.

WORKING WITHIN A BUDGET

The longer I'm in Europe shopping, the more cautious I have to be about money, because after days of dealing with figures and negotiating prices, I become desensitized and money itself starts to lose its importance. If you'll be doing this for any length

Markets in Italy, like the monthly antiques fair in Arezzo, which boasts four hundred vendors, tend to feel a little more relaxed than their French counterparts, but be prepared for extended negotiations—Italians hate to part with their furniture!

of time it's important to establish a budget and have a daily check-in to see where you are and what you've got left to spend. Knowing what you can and want to pay will make the process of negotiating easier, too (more on that below).

SHIPPING

If you're shopping for anything other than "smalls" (industry speak for little accessories and decorative objects), you'll need to ship things home, and the good news is that there's an infrastructure set up for that. In the Paris flea markets and some of the bigger seasonal *déballages*, firms have stalls in the markets themselves and can ship anything from a single item to full containers. But if you're on a larger buying trip it's generally easier to arrange your shipper beforehand, especially if you'll be shopping at markets or fairs outside Paris or in Italy where that kind of service can be harder to find. An Internet search for antiques shippers will yield plenty of options.

The shipping company will give you a buying book where you'll list your purchases as well as contact information for the vendor, and then it'll take it from there. Keep in mind that rates are somewhat negotiable and, as with buying items at a flea market, the more you buy—or in this case, the more you ship—the better the rate you are likely to get. Always opt for insurance on air or container shipping—rough seas and containers overboard are not unheard-of, and there are plenty of other pitfalls that could otherwise spell disaster.

The easiest point of entry for most beginners in Europe is the flea markets, and a key to shopping them is understanding how they work. What I quickly learned when starting out myself is that there's a food chain, especially in Paris. It starts with the markets at the bottom of the chain—places like the Jules Vallès *puce* or nearby *entrepôts*, some of the many such markets generally considered part of the Marché aux Puces de Saint-Ouen in the north of the city. I'd see even high-end dealers shopping these markets early in the morning—I'm talking five or six A.M., when vendors are just unloading their trucks. These guys are unpacking their *camion* in the dark, and the high-end dealers are right there, buying pieces as they come off the vehicle. At Jules Vallès or other no-frills *entrepôts*, an object might be one hundred euros, but it won't be for long, and its ultimate price depends on where it ends up. If it goes to Vernaison, another *puce*, it might only double in price. If it goes to Paul Bert, it might go up by three or four times. If it goes to Serpette, it might be priced at five to ten times the initial price. From there it might go to a blue-chip shop near the Louvre or on the Left Bank, and I guarantee it'll definitely end up with a price tag that's well above one hundred euros.

The thing to keep in mind, then, is that everyone is shopping the same sources, and with every exchange, the price goes up. If you want the best possible deals, you have to get up early, get to places like the smaller *entrepôts*, where the *camions* are unloading, and dive in. When I'm in Europe I go to bed and wake up at the same time as the *grand-mères* motivated by the dread of

potentially seeing a piece that would have made my day disappear into another dealer's container.

The scene on the ground that early is not for the faint of heart, however. This is not the moment to meditate on whether you really like something or not because there's going to be someone right behind you with his or her wallet already out. Of course, there are plenty of people who prefer the relatively low-pressure scene later in the day at markets like Paul Bert or Serpette and that's perfectly fine, but understanding how the markets work will give you insight into the veiled arena of price and value, which is always a good thing.

NAVIGATING (AND NEGOTIATING) IN THE FLEA MARKETS

The first thing you'll realize in a flea market is that nothing has a price tag on it. You *always* have to ask. And remember, you'll possibly be given the number based on your attire, your handbag, your shoes, your coat. Leave the jewelry and the statement handbag at home. I usually wear jeans and wellies (you're constantly being caught in some weather situation or another, no matter the time of year), a nondescript coat, and a hat. And while many vendors these days accept credit cards, cash is still king. It'll always get you a better deal. Get a money belt, put it on under your shirt or sweater, and

have those euros on hand.

Weekdays are also better for flea markets than weekends, at least those that operate more regularly. On the weekends, especially Sundays, vendors will take the day off and hire someone to man their stall. It's an awkward day to negotiate. The representatives will have a set price for the merchandise and *maybe* 10 percent wiggle room—if you need them to go lower, they'll have to call the vendor and they won't always be able to reach them. Go on a Thursday, Friday, or Saturday, when you'll meet the person in charge.

If I see something I like at a stall, the first thing I do is scan the rest of the merchandise—a lot of times, you get a better price if you buy a bundle of items rather than just one. Either way, I'm trying not to look too interested. Even if I really, really want something I play it cool. (Give off an I've-got-to-have-this vibe and you're probably not going to get a good deal.) I try to speak the language, whether it's French or Italian (even learning just a few important terms helps), and ask the price.

The minute you query a vendor for how much they want for something, they might try to get *you* to name *your* price and my number-one rule is never throw out a price. I just say, "Oh no, you, please," and I work that until I put it firmly back on them. My philosophy on negotiating is whoever throws out the price first, yields. The less you reveal the better.

Accomplishing that, if the stated quote is fair, within my budget, and close enough to the figure I had in my head, I welcome the offer. Accept what's fair. Vendors have to make a living, too. It's ultimately a small community, and if you're committed to antiques,

ABOVE: A nineteenth-century candelabra with gilded vintage iron I found in Arezzo; lighting is a strong suit of the Italian markets. **OPPOSITE**: Browsing architectural salvage materials at another *entrepôt* off the rue de Rosiers. My inconspicuous outfit is not an accident. It's best to dress down while you are working in the field.

there will always be a next time. You *always* get a more favorable outcome if they like and respect you. It changes the dynamic.

If the price is more than I want to pay, I say something about how beautiful the piece is and how sorry I am that it's out of my budget. Then I ask if there's a better price. Again, they'll probably ask what I'm willing to pay and again I refuse—politely—to state a number. Replying, "Please, it's *your* furniture, *you* tell me." Once that happens and I see that the person is really willing to negotiate, then I might go in and say, "Will you take X for this piece?" That number is *not* lower than the number I'm ultimately willing to pay—in other words, not a lowball offer. I always put my best foot forward. In all the years I've been doing this, the tactic has never led me astray.

Some etiquette pointers: Never interrupt somebody else's negotiation, even though there might be a lot of people interested in the same piece. Let them do their thing. If they walk away, you can immediately walk in and start. (It's also a good thing to keep in mind if you're negotiating over something you really want, because the moment you turn your back on it somebody can swoop in and pick it up.)

Negotiating varies, country to country, too. In France, it's usually a faster process. The French tend to be more transaction-oriented and they definitely have more stock—for them, it's about turning over inventory. In Italy, it's a whole different story. They don't have as much stock, there's not a ton of Americans buying there, and they are in *love* with their furniture. They have the hardest time parting with it much like me. They are trying *not* to sell it to you, frankly. Either it's the best act I've ever seen or they're really, really attached to their antiques. Unless money is no object, factor in a longer negotiating time.

The Paul Bert *puce* in Paris on a weekday, when the owners of the stalls are on duty so you can readily negotiate.

SHOP OWNERS NEGOTIATE, TOO

You might think that a dealer with a proper storefront or a blue-chip address might be above negotiating, but I have to tell you, I've shopped in all kinds of places, even in the top echelons of the food chain, and come out smiling. It really depends on the mood of the shop owner or the dealer and a million other factors you can't predict: Maybe they've just been audited, or made a great sale and are feeling generous, or the piece you like has been stuck on the sales floor for years. Maybe they just need the cash and, lucky you, you have plenty in your money belt.

I remember one of my first buying trips. I made friends with this fellow from London, and we were browsing some high-end shops. Charlie was in the market for some serious pieces—let's say he was ready to buy a $30,000 console—and he let me piggyback on his purchase. The dealer gave *me* a deal because Charlie gave him such a huge sale. (Of course, my purchase was nowhere near as extravagant!)

What I learned from the experience is that you can really negotiate anywhere. You go in with the same attitude. If you're in love with something and can't live without it, ask the owner for the best price. Ask what the price would be if you're paying cash. It's a one-on-one negotiation, especially if you're dealing with the proprietor and they're simpatico. You never know unless you ask.

THE PARIS *PUCES*

The Paris flea markets are where most serious antiques collectors cut their teeth, and with good reason: The selection is a constant flow of some of the best stock in the world, with a strength, unsurprisingly, in the popular French eras (but I've found amazing things from a wide range of cultures and time periods). The majority of these markets are concentrated in Saint-Ouen, a neighborhood in the north of the city, just beyond the Périphérique (the road that encircles central Paris), above the 17th and 18th arrondissements. They're accessible by the Metro, but these days I find Uber to be the easiest and safest bet (the areas you have to traverse immediately around the train stations can be a little sketchy). Be vigilant: Pickpockets are a real threat (another reason to pack a money belt).

Here's an overview of my favorites, highlighting what kind of antiques each is good for. Bear in mind there are no secret sources or a web of under-the-radar dealers that professionals have special access to. Just because a vendor had a gorgeous Gustavian bench on one visit doesn't mean they'll have a great selection of Gustavian pieces on your next trip. It's always hit-or-miss, and you never know what you're going to find until you show up. General information on all the *puces* can be found through the Marché aux Puces de Paris/ Saint-Ouen's Website: *marcheauxpuces-saintouen.com.*

MARCHÉ BIRON. Two long aisles where you can find pieces from the eighteenth century through art deco and where I have purchased large nineteenth-century paintings and other unexpected finds. *85 rue des Rosiers, Saint-Ouen; marchebiron.com.*

MARCHÉ DAUPHINE. Vintage midcentury pieces, eighteenth-nineteenth century furnishings, and garden elements. *132–40 rue des Rosiers, Saint-Ouen; marche-dauphine.com.*

MARCHÉ JULES VALLÈS. A no-frills market that's good for smalls (accessories like single chairs, candlesticks, and jewelry) and bargain hunters who don't mind showing up at the crack of dawn. *7 rue Jules Vallès, Saint-Ouen; paulbert-serpette.com/en/marche-jules-valles.*

MARCHÉ MALASSIS. Vintage and antique jewelry, art deco, and fine art. *142 rue des Rosiers, Saint-Ouen; marchemalassis.com.*

MARCHÉ PAUL BERT. Small- to medium-sized furniture and accessories (consistently a staple source for me). *96–110, rue des Rosiers, Saint-Ouen; paulbert-serpette.com.*

MARCHÉ AUX PUCES DE LA PORTE DE VANVES. Accessories, antique books, porcelain and ceramics, and vintage clothing. Unlike the others, Porte de Vanves is on the south side of Paris, near the 14th arrondissement. *Avenue Marc Sangnier and Avenue Georges Lafenestre; pucesdevanves.fr.*

MARCHÉ SERPETTE. Adjacent to the larger Paul Bert, the smaller Serpette has a vetted inventory spanning all eras from the seventeenth to twentieth centuries, including vintage pieces by known designers. *96–110, rue des Rosiers, Saint-Ouen; paulbert-serpette.com.*

MARCHÉ VERNAISON. Runs the gamut from smalls to case goods. Always good for unexpected treasures. *99 rue des Rosiers, Saint-Ouen; vernaison.com.*

ABOVE: A stall specializing in lighting fixtures at Paul Bert, which is also excellent for decorative accessories and "smalls." Shopping at flea markets is an exercise in opportunism—you never know what you're going to find, so you can't have a single focus; keep your eyes peeled and you may find a diamond to bring home. OPPOSITE: A nineteenth-century Italian table and a nineteenth-century iron garden urn at an *entrepôt.*

DÉBALLAGES AND OTHER SHOPPING OUTSIDE PARIS

Outside of Paris there are fairs, or *déballages*, going on all the time. Some of them, like the one in Lyon, are permanent, open every weekend, and function much like a Paris *puce* would. Others, like the one in Montpellier, happen at set times of year and draw dealers and professionals from all over Europe and beyond. There are also specific regions, like the South of France, where there are lots of little towns within easy driving distance of one another that have great markets and shops and can yield surprising finds. Seasonal *déballages* aside, these venues are less competitive than those in Paris, but prices tend to be higher—they just don't have the traffic or turnover.

GENERAL RESOURCES

The following Websites will be helpful in finding regional flea markets and *déballages* throughout France and in Italy, my two main stomping grounds: fleamarketinsiders.com; fleamapket.com; francebrocante.fr (an aggregator of sites to search for *déballages*); and francebrocante.fr (the site's in French and you'll need to search by region, so have a map handy).

LYON

When you've exhausted the markets in the capital, hop on a train and go to Lyon for the day. It has a set area where the exhibitors show every Friday, Saturday, and Sunday (arrive on Thursday evening so you can start bright and early on Friday). The city of Lyon has a good selection of dealers, too, so when you're done at the fair you can walk from warehouse to warehouse to warehouse; see pucesducanal.com for details.

SOUTH OF FRANCE

Provence has its own *puces* and dealers and is a great home base to explore the surrounding towns (many of which also host regular markets as well as seasonal *déballages*), including Avignon, L'Isle sur la Sorgue, Pézenas, and Béziers. The South is a particularly good resource for architectural materials salvaged from old estates and houses: fireplaces, roof tiles, floor tiles, bathroom tiles, boiserie, fountains, and garden elements. You'll see *entrepôts*, or warehouses, for salvaged materials in all of these towns—when you see signs that say *antiquaire*, *antiquités*, or *matériaux anciens*, pull over. And check in at local tourism offices; many small towns publish a list of *entrepôts* in their area.

STRATEGIES FOR SEASONAL DÉBALLAGES

Seasonal fairs or *déballages* happen all the time, all over France, and are usually held in open fields. There are popular ones in Chartres, Le Mans, Béziers, Montpellier, and Lille.

Shopping at seasonal *déballages* is a contact sport akin to shopping the most competitive Paris flea markets in early mornings, when the trucks are unloading. They work at a rapid pace. Most of them begin at eight in the morning, and much of the major trading happens in the first hour. And it's a lot of ground to cover—usually seven or eight halls plus an exterior perimeter lined with dealers that can't afford to be inside. Scan stalls quickly and keep moving. The key is commitment. If you see

something you like and it speaks to you, negotiate, settle on a price, and buy it. I still dream about this chandelier that I lost to another dealer in Montpellier because it might have been a hundred euros more than I wanted to spend and I hesitated. The moment you walk away another person will walk right in.

My best strategy is to carry a notebook and mark down the stand number and negotiated price of items I'm on the fence about. Chances are they won't be there when I return, but at least I'll know where the dealer and I left off in case they are.

ITALY

Antiques shopping in Italy can be a far more relaxed affair than it is in France. For starters, as I've said before, there aren't a lot of Americans in these markets, so competition isn't as intense. Generally speaking, the country is an excellent resource for lighting—chandeliers, sconces, candelabras—and decorative accessories like candlesticks and reliquaries. I have found gorgeous furniture there, too, but not reliably. It's hard to pigeonhole individual fairs by what they might be known for because it is truly the luck of the draw. That makes Italy a slightly riskier proposition than shopping in France, because the shopping is really unpredictable, but if you are there for buying (or eating!) it's always an adventure. The weekend markets, when vendors set up at tables in beautiful piazzas, are my preference. I jump on a bike and go. Here are my favorite towns to shop and what to look for in each.

AREZZO. Antique jewelry, sets of antique to vintage chairs. *Last Saturday and first Sunday of the month; fieraantiquaria.org.*

CUNEO. Headboards, Tuscan doors, garden elements; furniture tends to have darker finishes. *Last Saturday of the month; comune.cuneo.it.*

FOSSANO. I've found eighteenth-century tables and lighting, but have also come up empty-handed. *Third Sunday of the month from March through May and September through October; comune.fossano.cn.it.*

GENOA. Eighteenth- to nineteenth-century chandeliers, tables, and bedroom furniture. *First weekend of the month; genovantiquaria.com.*

LUCCA. Small decorative items, occasionally Tuscan buffets and credenzas. *Third weekend of the month; www.comune.lucca.it/Mercato_Antiquario.*

MODENA. Mostly eighteenth- to nineteenth-century decorative accessories (though once I was fortunate to find a seventeenth-century *faux bois* armoire). *Last weekend of the month; visitmodena.it/it/da-non perdere/antiquariato.*

PARMA. High-end fair with goods from the seventeenth to twentieth centuries. *Thursdays; turismo.comune.parma.it.*

ABOVE: A plaster statue purchased in the South of France, where garden elements and salvaged architectural materials like roof and floor tiles, fireplaces, brick, and boiserie are particularly plentiful at markets and *entrepôts*. OPPOSITE: Inspecting a pair of Directoire stools at an *entrepôt* in Saint-Ouen.

AUCTION HOUSES

For those who hit a wall at the Paris *puces* or find prices too high for their tastes, the intrepid can try their hand at the Drouot auction house in the center of the city (drouot.com). It hosts seventy independent firms across sixteen halls and there's always an auction going on in the afternoon. The proceedings will be in French, but you can raise your hand and say, "*En anglais si'l vous plaît*," and the auctioneer will be compelled to translate. Be prepared for the looks you'll get: The faces around you will belong to the owners of the stalls in many of the flea markets, and while they might love you when you're browsing their wares in Saint-Ouen, at Drouot, their stares might not be as friendly. If you would rather shop under the radar, you can always just leave a bid. Find one of the men in red coats that work for the firm and tell them your outside bid on a particular item, then check back later and be prepared to alert your shipper if you won. You have a certain period of time to pick up the merchandise before you start incurring storage fees.

Thanks to the Internet, you don't have to go all the way to Paris to take advantage of the auction scene. One of my favorite resources is Live Auctioneers (liveauctioneers.com), which lists live sales at smaller regional houses all across the United States and abroad. It's brilliant because you can search by item or period, and if the auction is not well attended, you can really do well.

SHOPPING GUIDE

UNITED STATES
EASTERN

ISTDIBS GALLERY. More than fifty exhibitors. *269 11th Ave, Lobby 4, 7th Floor, New York, NY 10001. 1stdibs.com*

ANTIQUE & DESIGN CENTER OF HIGH POINT. More than sixty-five dealers. *Twice a year. Historic Market Square 316 W Commerce Ave High Point, NC 27260. hpadc.com*

BRIMFIELD ANTIQUE SHOW. More than 5,000 dealers stretched along one mile of Route 20, MA. *Three times a year. brimfieldshow.com*

NEW HAMPSHIRE ANTIQUES SHOW. More than sixty-eight dealers. *Three times a year. nhada.org*

NEW HAMPSHIRE'S ROUTE 4 ANTIQUE ALLEY. Five hundred dealers in twenty miles of shops. *Portsmouth, NH. nhantiquealley.com*

SCOTT ANTIQUE MARKET. 3,330 dealers. Three locations. *3650 and 3850 Jonesboro Rd SE, Atlanta, GA 30354, 717 E 17th Ave, Columbus, Ohio 43211, 213 Fairview Ave, Washington Court House, OH 43160. scottantiquemarket.com*

SPRINGFIELD OHIO ANTIQUE SHOW. More than two thousand dealers. *4401 S Charleston Pike, Springfield, OH 45502. springfieldantiqueshow.com*

SOUTH

ANTIQUES AT THE GARDENS. Once a year. *2612 Lane Park Road Birmingham, AL 35223. bbgardens.org/antiques.php*

MAGAZINE STREET. More than forty antique shops along six miles. *New Orleans, LA. magazinestreet.com*

THE ORIGINAL ROUND TOP ANTIQUES FAIR. More than 2,500 dealers. *Three times a year. 475 Texas Hwy 237 South, Carmine, TX 78932. roundtoptexasantiques.com*

THE ORIGINAL MIAMI BEACH ANTIQUE SHOW. More than seven hundred recognized dealers from thirty countries. *Once a year. 1901 Convention Center Drive, Miami Beach, Florida 33139. originalmiamibeachantiqueshow.com*

ROYAL STREET. Located in the French quarter, which is thirteen blocks full of antique shops. *New Orleans, LA. neworleans.com/things-to-do/shopping/antiques-shops*

MIDWEST

WALNUT ANTIQUE SHOW. More than three hundred dealers. *Once a year. Walnut is located in Iowa at exit 46 on I-80. walnutantiqueshow.com*

WEST COAST

ALAMEDA POINT ANTIQUES FAIRE. Eight hundred dealers. *First Sunday of each month; 2900 Navy Way, Alameda, CA 94501. alamedapointantiquesfaire.com*

SANTA MONICA AIRPORT OUTDOOR ANTIQUE & COLLECTIBLE MARKET. Spread across the tarmac of the local airport in Santa Monica, CA. *First and fourth Sunday every Month. 3050–3090 Airport Ave, Los Angeles, CA 90405. santamonicaairportantiquemarket.com*

ONLINE

ISTDIBS. Connect to the world's best dealers, finest shops, most important galleries and shop the most beautiful things on earth. *1stdibs.com*

ART-DESIGN-CARTA. A private marketplace available to art and design professionals that allows dealers to offer their latest finds before posting them on any open market sites. *artdesigncarta.com*

CHAIRISH. The world's first online consignment marketplace for design-obsessed people to buy and sell exceptional pre-owned home furnishings. Selection of fabulous home furnishings that come direct from the owner at a great price. *chairish.com*

DECASO. Short for the Decorative Arts Society, Decaso is a great online source for modernist and antique furniture, decor, and decorative art objectives. They have high standards of authenticity and curation and work directly with dealers to curate their online selection. *decaso.com*

DECORATIVE COLLECTIVE. Dealers from the UK and Europe selling antique, midcentury and vintage furniture, lighting, mirrors, art, and accessories for the home and garden. *decorativecollective.com*

PHILLIPS. Phillips is a four-generation-old family run business. The furniture selection is focused on objects from the colonial period and the art deco and midcentury era. Phillips has a selection of interesting and unusual pieces that would fit in both a traditional or modern interior of today. *phillipsantiques.com*

RUBY LANE. The world's largest curated marketplace for antiques, vintage collectibles, vintage fashion, fine art, and jewelry. *rubylane.com*

SOTHEBY'S HOME. The premier online consignment platform for buying and selling exceptional pre-owned furniture, antiques, vintage pieces, art, lighting, collections, and everything else found in stylish homes across the country. *sothebyshome.com*

AUCTIONS

BONHAMS. One of the largest companies of its kind in the United States and the third largest auction house in the world. Bonhams specializes in the appraisal and sale of fine art, antiques, and decorative objects in virtually every auction category. *bonhams.com*

CHRISTIE'S. Christie's is a British auction house founded in the eighteenth century. It is the most globally recognized seller of high-end, extremely rare original art, antiques, and collectibles. *christies.com*

DOYLE. Doyle is one of the world's foremost auctioneers and appraisers of fine art, jewelry, furniture, decorative arts, coins, Asian works of art, and a variety of specialty categories. *doyle.com*

HERITAGE AUCTIONS. The largest collectibles auctioneer and third largest auction house in the world, as well as the largest auction house founded in the US. Heritage is an auctioneer of numismatic collections, comics, fine art, books, luxury accessories, and memorabilia from film, music, history, and sports. *ha.com*

ACKNOWLEDGMENTS

INVALUABLE. Bid online in live auctions from all over the world. Browse fine and decorative art, antiques, estate jewelry, coins and stamps, collectibles, and more. *invaluable.com*

LIVE AUCTIONEERS. World's Largest art, antiques, and collectibles online marketplace. 280,000+ items for online auction from 4,000+ auctioneers. *liveauctioneers.com*

NYE & CO. Antiques and collectibles that will become your children's heirlooms, all within your budget. The bulk of business comes from the trust and estate community in the tri-state area, although they maintain relationships all over the country. *nyeandcompany.com*

SKINNER. Skinner attracts top consignments and commands record-breaking prices in the international auction marketplace. Offers more than sixty auctions annually. Skinner auctions reach an international audience and showcase the unique, rare, and beautiful in dozens of categories, including the fine and decorative arts, jewelry, modern design, musical instruments, science and technology, wine, and many others. *skinnerinc.com*

SOTHEBY'S. The 275-year-old auction house online marketplace is as luxurious as the items available for sale on it. One of the world's largest brokers of fine and decorative art, jewelry, real estate, and collectibles. *sothebys.com*

SUSANIN'S AUCTIONEERS & APPRAISERS. Auctions at Susanin's feature: American, English, and Continental furniture; decorative arts; rugs and carpets; Asian arts; fine paintings, prints, and sculptures; silver; fine jewelry and timepieces; couture; and accessories, coins, ephemera, collectibles, and more. *susanins.com*

ROLAND AUCTIONS NEW YORK. Conducts live and online auctions. Roland Auctions consistently offers an eclectic collection of period antiques and traditional-style furnishings, fine art, collectibles, oriental rugs, jewelry, items of virtue, and more. *rolandantiques.com*

A special thanks to all the patrons who have lined up and slept in front of my warehouse to get first dibs on a new shipment and then participated in the lottery system so they wouldn't have to sleep in front of the warehouse doors. Thanks as well to the many brave souls who took flights from other states in hopes of acquiring treasure. Without you, I would not have gotten up at four A.M. and gone searching with a flashlight for antiques dealers unloading their trucks, hitchhiked when I could not find a taxi, or slept in thirty-euro-a-night hotels. It has been my absolute pleasure to see people leaving my warehouse happier than they were when they came in and hearing stories of where the items landed. Without the support of the design and antiques community, I never would have been able to discover so many treasures and be exposed to them, even if only briefly, as they flowed through our doors.

To all the antiques dealers around the world from whom I purchased an endless parade of sublime objects, thanks for the never-ending adventure.

To Jill Cohen, who encouraged me to tell my story and fearlessly believed there was an audience for it.

To my office staff, who also believed we had a magical story to tell through antiques and design. Special thanks go to Analise Braisher Riggins, my design manager.

To the artisans in New Orleans, who make my hand-forged iron ideas come to life.

To RH, you validated me.

Thanks to art directors Doug Turshen and David Huang—you have made the creation of this book a pleasure and a joy.

To Mario López-Cordero, fellow whippet-lover and my source of daring vocabulary that I nevertheless made you dial back.

To Shawna Mullen and the Abrams team, who made this journey come to life with more flourish than I had imagined.

To all the clients that have trusted us with their pocketbooks and homes, the most rewarding compliment I've ever heard is, "I never want to leave home." You have made my heart overflow with gratitude and joy. Joie de vivre is actually what we sell.

To my church and spiritual best friend, Parris. Your encouragement and prayers have carried me through many a tunnel.

To my family, you emboldened me to live without limits. Without your love and support, I would not have had the courage to walk on water.

To my brilliant, kind, and handsome better half, I look forward to living in Europe with you, covered in fair dirt and spending all our free time at the *librarie*.